Bulbul Sharma is a painter and writer based in New Delhi. Her works are in the collection of the National Gallery of Modern Art, Lalit Kala Akademi and Chandigarh Museum as well as in private collections in India, UK, USA, Japan, Canada and France.

She has published several books which include the bestselling *Travels with My Aunt* and *The Anger of Aubergines.* Her books have been translated into Italian, French, German, Chinese, Spanish and Finnish.

Bulbul's books for children include *The Fabled Book of Gods and Demons* and *The Ramayana.*

AF652031

ALSO BY BULBUL SHARMA

The Perfect Woman
The Anger of Aubergines
Banana-Flower Dreams
The Book of Devi
Shaya Tales: Stories of a Himalayan Village
Eating Women, Telling Tales
Now That I'm Fifty: Stories of Women Who Have Scored Half a Century
Travels With My Aunt
Love and Learning Under the Magnolia
Murder at the Happy Home for the Aged
Murder in Shimla
Birds in My Garden And Beyond
Between Heaven and Earth: Writings on the Indian Hills (Edited with Ruskin Bond)
Sunbirds in the Morning, Hornbills at Dusk

Mayadevi's London Yatra

New and Selected Stories

BULBUL SHARMA

SPEAKING TIGER

SPEAKING TIGER BOOKS LLP
125A, Ground Floor, Shahpur Jat, Near Asiad Village,
New Delhi - 110 049

First published in paperback by Speaking Tiger Books in 2023

Copyright © Bulbul Sharma 2024

ISBN: 978-93-5447-882-6
eISBN: 978-93-5447-861-1

10 9 8 7 6 5 4 3 2 1

The moral right of the author has been asserted.

Typeset in Garamond by Jojy Philip
Printed at: Impressions Printing & Packaging Ltd., Noida

No part of this publication may be reproduced, transmitted, or stored in a retrieval system, in any form or by any means, electronic, mechanical, photocopying, recording or otherwise, without the prior permission of the publisher.

This book is sold subject to the condition that it shall not, by way of trade or otherwise, be lent, resold, hired out, or otherwise circulated, without the publisher's prior consent, in any form of binding or cover other than that in which it is published.

To the memory of late Dr Ashok Mukerjee,
the kindest brother I was fortunate to have…

Contents

1

Fish Curry Memories

A cool breeze, faintly smelling of damp leaves, touched her face as she walked, looking for an empty bench. Leela did not like sitting next to strangers, especially foreigners. 'I keep forgetting that I am the foreigner in this country and not them,' she said to herself, settling down on a bench near the pond. She loved being in the park at this time of the day, when it was not too crowded. Two young women strolled by, dressed in baggy black pants, heavy boots and jackets as if they were in training for serious combat and not just walking their dogs in the park.

When she had arrived in London a year ago, Leela used to feel odd walking in her sari and old-fashioned Bata shoes, but then she realized that nobody ever looked at her. They were all busy on their phones. Besides, people here dressed in all kinds of strange clothes. One day she had seen a man walking around in flowing saffron robes with a vermilion tilak on his forehead. He looked so much like their purohit at home except that he was blonde with blue eyes.

Leela suddenly felt a rush of homesickness as she thought about her little puja room at home. How she missed her silver idols—missed bathing them, dressing them, and cooking prasad for the various gods and goddesses. She knew they must be missing her too since there was no one at home to look after them in her absence.

Soon. She would be home soon, if all went well.

Leela started walking slowly towards the supermarket. She only had an hour to finish her chores before they came home. A woman passed her, shouting angrily to someone on her mobile phone. Leela always looked away when she talked on the mobile and it was just as well that hardly anyone called her. You could see a person's face in sharp focus now on the phones and this unnerved her. She did not like seeing people's faces up-close. They looked so ugly with all their blemishes magnified even on the small mobile screens—their eyes looked yellow, spots shone on their skin and their crooked teeth flashed with an evil gleam.

Her nephew Manu, with whom she lived here, had given her his old phone though his wife had scolded him about it. She was always screaming at him about something or the other. He would listen quietly for a little while and then suddenly flare up and shout back. They bickered all the time or sat silently staring at their laptops. Manu, it seemed, had lost his job a few years ago and Nisha harangued him for not making enough effort to find another one. It was not a happy home and its sadness touched Leela too.

Manu often complained to Leela about his wife. 'No pleasing this woman. I try and try but fail. She was so sweet and gentle when I first met her but now she has turned into a witch,' he had said to her the other day when Nisha was not at home.

Leela had made a spicy fish curry and Monu had made some rice in a bag in the microwave. It tasted like the leftover, stale rice they had at home sometimes. 'This is like panta bhaat and we can have it with lemon,' she had said but Monu had no idea what she was talking about and just nodded as he ate the fish curry messily with his fingers, a distracted look in his eyes.

Monu and his so-difficult-to-please wife, Nisha, had come to live in the UK more than ten years ago. He was Leela's late sister's son—her only child. Leela had looked after him when he was a little boy since her sister, a doctor, often worked late at the hospital. He used to call her Ma-masi, following her around all day, holding on to her sari-pallav, but now he only called her Masi or nothing at all.

She had been surprised when he had sent her a ticket last year, asking her to come to London for a few months. 'Ma has gone and you are all alone in that big house. You should come and live with us for a little while,' he had said on the phone. He had called on the landline phone so she had not seen his face. Maybe if she had, she would not have come to London. She would have seen that he did not really want her; he needed a servant.

Leela got up at dawn every day and bathed and dressed as quietly as she could since she did not want to disturb them. After Nisha left for office and Monu went job hunting, she cleaned the flat, cooked a meal for Monu and herself since Nisha hardly ever ate at all. Then she washed and ironed their clothes, watered the plants and twice a week she went out to do all the grocery shopping. Sometimes Manu came with her but she preferred to go on her own since he always wanted to stop at a place called the pub which was crowded with young people drinking and talking loudly. 'Just one quick drink,' he would say, looking at her with pleading eyes, like he had done as a child.

At first Leela could not do anything right and had made a mess in the flat by switching on the wrong button on the washing machine and flooding the kitchen. Then she had burnt the food while cooking on the glass stove that had no flame, setting the fire alarm off. Slowly, after a few months, Leela had learnt how to manage the house. At home she had done everything so well, so effortlessly. She had looked after her aged parents and then cared for her ailing sister but she had had servants to help her. And, now in this unfriendly, unfamiliar home, she had become a servant in her old age.

Leela felt like a prisoner under house arrest and she often lay awake in her tiny bedroom, staring at the walls in the darkness. How had she got trapped like this? She could not return home since she had no money and Monu had put her passport 'safely' away somewhere. 'Why do you need it? It is safe with me. As soon as I get a job, we will both go to India,' he said to her every time she asked for her passport. Leela knew now that he had been without a job for three years.

Then one day it all changed.

She met Mira.

A raven suddenly flew across her path and Leela smiled as she walked towards the park gates from the main streets. The day she had met Mira in this very park, a raven had come and perched near them. The bird looked like a crow but its black feathers had a beautiful sheen that the poor, drab-looking crows at home did not have.

When Leela reached home, carrying a heavy load of groceries, Nisha was already there, sipping green tea in the kitchen. She gave her a quick glance but did not offer to help. Then she went to her bedroom and slammed the door shut. Leela put everything away like Monu had showed her and started the evening meal. She wondered once more where Manu spent the whole day, since she knew he still had not found a job. Maybe at that place he called 'pub'.

It was 7 o'clock. She only had three hours to wait. She would clean the kitchen, put away the dishes and say goodnight to Monu and Nisha, though they never looked up from their laptops to say goodnight to her. Then she would steal out of the main door, as quiet as a thief, and go downstairs. Her feet, clad in rubber slippers, made a faint, squelching sound on the uncarpeted floor but there was no one in this, vast empty basement area to hear it.

Leela pushed open the door to the tiny, dimly lit room and the smell of spices greeted her like an old friend.

Mira, waiting by the window, looked up with a smile.

For the next three hours, Leela cooked at top speed. She ground spices, kneaded dough, stirred the masalas and cooked large quantities of curry. A row of dishes sat on the counter, waiting to be filled with freshly made food, while a pile of different kinds of parathas soon stacked up on the shelf. Mira now got busy chopping onions, her eyes watering.

'The bus was so crowded today and my bag of groceries burst open, but one old English chap very kindly helped me pick up all the tomatoes,' said Mira, laughing.

'English people seem very polite and helpful,' said Leela, though she had never spoken to a single English person in the one year that she had been in London, except the immigration officer at the airport. But he had looked like an Indian, in fact, he had looked exactly like her neighbour's plump, curly-haired son except that he spoke like an Englishman.

'Leela Masi, will you make baigan bharta tomorrow? Special request from three people. Also, there are five orders for your potato and cauliflower sabzi,' said Mira, reading out a list. Leela nodded as she sprinkled freshly roasted cumin powder on the curry simmering on the stove.

She had been cooking secretly at night for three months now. Mira brought in the orders and she also bought all the vegetables, fish and chicken from a supermarket that was much cheaper. Once Leela had made the food, Mira packed it in plastic boxes to deliver to various homes.

~

It all began when Leela and Mira had met one day in the park by sheer chance and had started chatting about life in a foreign country and soon they had become friends, though Mira was several years younger than Leela.

'That curry smells so good. How do you do it? Is there magic in your hands?' asked Mira, and Leela gave her a quick, grateful look. She had cooked all her life but people had very rarely praised her. She knew they liked the food she prepared and kept asking for more but no one ever said anything; not a single word of praise had ever come her way. Mira's kind words pleased her so much, it was as if she had received a surprise gift.

It was Mira who had thought up this midnight cooking scheme and convinced Leela to do it. Mira worked as a maid, cleaning and doing household chores for various people in the building. She had a small apartment in the basement. Her kitchen was tiny but Leela found her old gas stove much easier to use than the gleaming black glass stove in Manu's flat that kept blinking angrily at her. Mira's battered stove reminded her of the temperamental stove at home which would often flare up for no reason at all and then calm down a few minutes later.

Mira paid Leela generously for all the food she cooked for delivery every night and only kept a small amount from whatever money they made. Leela had told her to take some extra payment for the ingredients, but Mira had refused. 'You need the money more than I do, Masi. We have to get you home.' After three months of secret cooking, she now had almost enough money saved to buy a one-way ticket to Delhi. Leela was pleased and surprised to find that people here seemed to love her food, not just people in the building, but from homes where Mira worked too. More and more orders came in every day and the tin box where they kept their earnings, was now slowly filling with notes. Manu and Nisha, of course, had no idea of this and Leela hoped they would not find out till she had earned enough to go home.

~

Today they had seven orders for chicken curry and five orders for bhindi masala. 'You are a star, Masi. You know, everyone misses their mother's cooking here and you have a mother's touch,' Mira said, handing her a plate of chopped onions to fry.

'I always cooked at home though we had a cook. My sister, Monu's mother, was the smart one. She went to college, became a doctor. I was not too bright so I stayed at home and cooked for everyone. After I got married I cooked for my in-laws and though my mother-in-law criticized every mouthful she ate, she insisted that I make all her food. She would say to me, "I ask you only because I don't know what caste this new cook belongs to." Even though she was almost ninety, the old lady had a healthy appetite and loved fried food and her last words to me were, "Make potato cutlets for me again tomorrow but make them bigger,"' said Leela, with a wistful smile.

Mira nodded as she sliced the bhindi. 'One Indian lady I work for has three samosas and four chocolate digestive biscuits for tea every day. She is ninety-seven and full of energy,' said Mira.

'My late husband only ate what I cooked but like his mother, he too complained after every meal. "Leela, you will kill me one day with your rich curries," he used to say. Poor man. He did die suddenly one day but not after eating what I had made. He choked on a tandoori chicken leg at a restaurant,' said Leela.

Though she found cooking till midnight tiring and her back often ached during the day, she loved chatting to Mira. Leela did not feel shy talking to Mira about her life and it seemed as if she had known her for a long time.

It was so comforting to talk to someone, to hear a real person's voice. Though Manu was always asleep on the sofa with the television on, the flat seemed empty, as if no one had ever lived here. She knew Mira liked her company too, even though she was so much older than her. She could have been her daughter if she had ever had a child.

Mira had had a tough life ever since she had been abandoned by her husband as soon as she arrived in London as a young bride, but she was a brave girl. Despite being a graduate, she now worked as a maid and was not ashamed about it. Mira was also saving money to go home and said, 'I want to go back like a queen, with lots of expensive presents for my family. I don't want them to feel sorry for me.' Mira laughed when she said this but Leela noticed her eyes were glistening with tears. Mira, despite her cheerful smiles, had within her a core of sadness that Leela sometimes glimpsed in her eyes. Both Mira and Nisha had been disappointed in their marriages but unlike Nisha, Mira had not allowed herself to become bitter. Nisha's resentment and anger were forever simmering under her skin, making her lash out at the world.

'Raining again today and looks as if it will continue all day,' said Mira. 'At home how happy we used to feel when it rained. I would quickly fry pakoras for everyone,' said Leela.

'Here, we could be eating pakoras every day—morning, noon and night,' said Mira as the little kitchen, filled with the heady aroma of spices, echoed with their happy laughter.

Leela covered the pan to allow the chicken curry to simmer and began frying the bhindi she had cut in tiny pieces. It was a dish she had never made before but Mira had brought her the recipe from a friend.

'"Midnight cooks", that is what we could have called our company if we had ever set up one. Maybe you can come back next year and stay with me and cook away once again. Though I am not sure what we are doing is exactly legal,' said Mira. Leela shook her head, 'Never. I will never step out of India again once I get back. Anyway, I think my visa expired long ago and they won't allow me to come into this country again, thank God. No, Mira. You come to India and stay with me,' said Leela, patting her hand. 'Maybe I will find a good husband for you in my neighbourhood.'

'No thanks. I have no desire to ever marry again. I still have to get rid of one absconding husband,' said Mira, her voice sounding harsh and Leela knew she had made a mistake and touched a sensitive point in Mira's forever cheerful, confident persona.

'Can you guess how many shoes Nisha has in her shoe cupboard?' asked Leela, hoping to cheer up Mira.

'Must be a hundred. These rich women shop all the time. It makes them feel good. One lady I work for has twenty stuffed toys for her dog.'

'I don't think Manu and Nisha are rich. They are always arguing about money. I wish the poor boy would find a job. It is humiliating for a man to live on his wife's earnings.'

They had finished packing the food and were sitting at Mira's small dining table, sipping milky, sweet cardamom tea. 'I will get your ticket next week. I know a maid who knows how to book tickets on the computer. She has a laptop. I am saving up to buy one too,' said Mira.

Finally, they had 990 pounds and a bit more was still owed to them for a dozen bottles of tomato chutney Leela had made. After paying for her one way ticket to India, there was enough money left to buy Mira a laptop. Last week Leela had found her passport hidden in a drawer and had quietly begun packing her few belongings and storing them in a small bag Mira had given her, since her own battered suitcase had been thrown away by Nisha long ago.

Five cotton saris, five petticoats, four blouses and one shawl along with her prayer book. The only thing new she had was a white sweater Monu had bought for her when it started getting cold. She had hardly ever gone out then and Monu ordered the groceries to be delivered. 'Cheaper than buying her an expensive overcoat,' she had heard Nisha whisper.

'Your meanness knows no bounds,' Monu had hissed back.

'Look who is talking. I am the one breaking my back at a boring job while you hang out with your friends all day. You have one doting old woman cooking, cleaning and ironing for you and a wife paying all the bills. What are you complaining about?' Nisha had retorted in a low, angry voice

'I am trying to get a job. You know that,' Manu had said.

'For three years? Obviously, not trying hard enough. I have to pay for everything and now feed this aunt of yours too. You are nothing but a spoilt, overgrown baby. Grow up,' Nisha had sneered and then shut the bedroom door. The apartment fell silent.

Leela often wondered what she had done to make Nisha dislike her so much but then she decided that it was something from their past lives. 'I have to live through it; bear it somehow.' But when she mentioned this to Mira, the girl had glared angrily and said, 'This Nisha woman seems like a real nasty sourpuss. She is so mean to you and to her poor husband. Why is she so angry with everyone?'

'At home we would call her "one who has a boil on her bottom",' said Leela and felt a twinge of guilt as they both roared with laughter. 'She gets tired, probably, working long hours,' she added.

'I work from 6 a.m. till midnight but I don't rage at everyone. Probably because I have no one to vent to,' muttered Mira, stacking up the boxes in her bag.

On her last evening, Leela made a pungent mustard fish curry and served it to Monu with fluffy, fragrant rice she had freshly made, not the boil-in-bag kind. 'What is this?' said Nisha, sniffing the air like an angry cat.

'Fish curry, can't you see?' said Monu, in a surprisingly loud voice.

'I am having a beetroot salad,' said Nisha.

'Try a little. It is not often that you taste what I cook. God knows when I will make it again. Here let me serve you,' said Leela, no longer feeling afraid of Nisha now that she was leaving.

Nisha gave her a strange look and then suddenly turned and pounced on the dish like a starving person. She heaped rice on her plate and then poured a ladleful of fish curry on it. She shut her eyes and began eating with her fingers, as Monu and Leela watched in amazement.

'Oh. So good. I will regret it later. But it is so good. Thank you. This reminds me of home,' she said with an awkward smile. Monu gave her a surprised look, grunted and continued to eat, making a mess on the dining table but Nisha, for once, ignored it. She took another helping of fish curry. Leela noticed that for the first time, they looked at each other and smiled as they ate. The room became alive with the sound of three people eating noisily. Manu started telling them about his latest job interview, making them laugh. It was almost as if they were back at home, a family eating together, talking loudly, all at the same time.

'Whatever bad karma had been there between them, the mustard fish curry has erased it,' thought Leela as she boarded the flight home. She wished Nisha would smile at Manu more often. She looked so beautiful when she did. In the evening, when they both returned home, they would find her letter. She would be far, far away in the sky by then. They would be furious with her since she had left without telling them, but there was enough left over fish curry to atone for what she had done. She had already forgiven them for how they had treated her since they were her only family; the only people who would remember her after she died. 'I am sure they will,' said Leela to herself as she looked out from the window at the clouds floating by.

2

Food to Die For

My grandmother fretted over everything. But a few weeks before my grandfather's shradh she would go into a major flap. Her two favourite worries were cleaning the house and cooking a special meal for the occasion. The third source of anxiety—finding a priest to feed—she kept in reserve so that she could give it her full, undivided, frenzied attention. The house, already as clean as a well-kept hospital ward, was now filled with the heady aroma of phenyl.

'Did you get the "lampblack" one?' she would ask Gopal the servant boy, suspiciously, about a particular brand of phenyl, as she could not read English. Then, holding the bottle under her nose, she would take a sniff as if it were vintage brandy. The room where my grandfather's annual shradh ceremony was to take place was swabbed and swept till bits of cement began to come off the ancient mosaic floor and were collected by the servant as concrete proof of his tireless effort. Each day I thought that Gopal, a young boy of fifteen, would protest and throw down his duster and broom. But he did not. Instead, he became even more frantic as the days went by, sweeping and cleaning like a man possessed. He crashed into furniture and tripped over tables as he swept the floor with his phenyl-drenched cloth, snarling at anyone who came in the way of his octopus-like crawl across the floor. No one was allowed into the shradh room except my grandmother and him. In the afternoons, when the rest of the house was asleep, I would see my grandmother sitting with Gopal on the floor in a corner of that vast room. Whispering like two conspirators, they searched for any hidden trails of dust. They were hysterical one day when they found that a sparrow had flown in while Gopal was not on guard and had left three tell-tale blobs on the floor.

'Maybe it is a good omen,' said Gopal, trying to avoid blame.

The cleaning phase finally ended. Then began the food phase. The main items on the menu, kheer, puri and potato curry remained fixed, but two new dishes had to be planned. The whole family debated this issue.

'Make gobhi. Dadaji liked it,' said my brother with a selfish desire for cauliflower.

'No, he did not, it gave him wind,' said my grandmother.

'Let us have carrot and peas then,' my father said.

'Carrots! Are my relatives rabbits that I should feed them carrots? And what will the priest think? We will make phulmakhani and paneer curry,' she said decisively and the subject was closed.

Gopal and my grandmother had already begun preparing the ingredients for each dish. Almonds and raisins had been washed till they lay pale and wan on the plates, huge quantities of best quality basmati rice had been scanned for hidden stones, and potatoes had been selected with the same sharp-eyed scrutiny as she had chosen brides for her sons. With only one day left for the shradh, the kitchen was now reserved for this exclusively. Some eager relatives had already begun to arrive. As soon as the women stepped into the house, they plunged right in, without being asked, to help with the preparations. They took off their slippers, washed their hands and sat down on the kitchen floor. Within minutes they were working in perfect coordination with my grandmother, yet I never heard her give them any instructions. Though they worked quietly, once in a while someone would offer a tidbit of interesting news for the group.

'Meera bhabi has had another girl,' and a collective sigh would go up. 'Ramlalji's house was sold for one crore,' would bring a gasp of amazement. Some remarks were perennial favourites and repeated every year. 'Bibiji, your eyes can pick out even the tiniest of stones from the rice,' a cousin would say and my grandmother would lob back her set answer, 'We ate pure ghee and in our youth there was no TV to make our eyes water.'

Another regular one, a favourite with the old lady was, 'Maaji, how do you keep the house so clean?'

'This boy helps but I have to watch out for any…,' she would say arching her eyebrows and throwing a swift glance in Gopal's direction and all the women and Gopal himself, understood the silent accusation.

This was the right time to start searching for the priest. Each woman gave her report about new priests they had seen at various weddings, funerals, shradhs, naming ceremonies and house-warming pujas. The height, weight and age, along with any other qualifying features, of each priest were related and my grandmother listened with rapt attention, her faded eyes gleaming like old silver. She rejected them all, one by one, and leaning against the kitchen wall began to cry, 'What will happen to his soul? How will I show my face in heaven when we meet?

Oh! Help me God, help to me to find the right one,' she sobbed while the women looked on in awe, their hands still busy peeling and chopping.

Last year's shradh was ruined for my grandmother because the priest would not eat anything at all. He pushed the kheer away because his blood sugar was high, and ate only two puris because his doctor had told him to avoid fat.

'Who has ever heard of a priest on a diet? What is the world coming to? Next they will ask for salad. How will they help me cross the river of death when my time comes, if they eat only boiled food?' my grandmother cried for days while we greedily lapped up the leftovers, including the priest's lion share.

Though the high point of the ceremony for my grandmother was feeding the priest, which would grant her many plus points in the scheme of heavenly merit, for the last ten years she had not found a man worthy of her culinary skills. Some were too bedraggled, and she suspected they were not genuine Brahmins because they had cracked, muddy feet.

'A real priest has feet as smooth and clean as a baby's since they are washed regularly,' she said. Others she rejected because they had a shifty look in their eyes which did not seem learned or high-born enough. One fellow who came to her door, smelling of cigarettes, was scolded and sent away in spite of having the advantage of bringing along his own cow for the shradh. Some were too fat for her liking, others too emaciated and sickly. One, to her horror, spoke in English and drove a car, while another did not know his Sanskrit well enough. Every year one member of the family was chosen by my grandmother to find the priest, and one by one we all failed her. This year her glance fell on me though I had been hiding from her eagle eyes.

'You know how to drive, you can go to the temples on the outskirts of the city and search. Remember to check that he doesn't have a blood sugar problem,' she ordered.

So I set off with a heavy heart, like a distraught prince who has been ordered by his bride's father to cross seven rivers, confront the giant, and bring back the lost jewel. At every temple I had to wait in a queue to meet the priest and when I finally reached the window where he was giving audience, he had already been taken.

'You understand, sister, how difficult it is for us to make everyone happy. We can eat only once a day. There are five of us here and we have been booked till the end of next month.'

I searched all day but could not find anyone to fit my grandmother's specifications. The ones that were available did not have the right weight, level of cleanliness and otherworldliness. One priest rejected our offer outright when he heard the menu—'too rich'; and another thought the offerings—'too little'; while a third agreed, but suddenly changed his mind and accepted the next, higher bid. Finally, when I was about to accept defeat and return home, an old priest took pity on me and brought out, from nowhere, a scrawny-looking boy.

The priest said, 'Take him, he is my son; but let me warn you, he is still a learner.'

The fledgling priest was all wrong, from his unkempt hair to Nike-clad feet, but my weary heart accepted him with humility.

I returned home in the evening to find cauldrons steaming and all the women chopping vegetables in a frenzy.

'Did you find him?' they asked eagerly. I nodded evasively and went out of the kitchen.

'What is he like?' my grandmother asked.

'He is young,' I replied truthfully.

'That is good. He will eat well and fearlessly. Maybe I should make one more vegetable. Gobhi will be good since he is young and will not worry about wind.' She turned away happily and called out to Gopal to buy five kilos of cauliflower. I was surprised that she did not ask for any more details. Her faith in my choice made me feel terribly ashamed about whom I had selected, and all night I lay awake afraid of what the next day would bring.

It was still dark when I heard my grandmother and Gopal in the kitchen. Gradually, as dawn began to break, the other women joined them. They worked silently in the dim light as if performing a secret ritual, their movements slow and precise and their silhouettes shifting and merging like ghosts dancing. The kheer bubbled and burped in a huge brass cauldron as Gopal stirred it continuously, the steam rising to cover his face with a fine mist. Two women sat on the floor with a flat plate of flour—while one kneaded the dough, the other kept pouring small amounts of water. They did not speak to each other but just nodded together every time the water was poured as if taking part in a pantomime. The vegetables which had already been chopped earlier were now thrown one by one into the kadai, along with spices, and the hot oil quickly changed their colours from pale green and white to deep red-brown. The final menu was potatoes in a rich, red gravy made only with tomatoes (no onions or garlic), cauliflower with just a dash of ginger to highlight its flavour, phulmakhani and paneer coated in a mild gravy, yogurt with a sprinkling of crisply fried boondi, and, of course, the mandatory kheer which was now going to simmer on a low fire till it turned a special shade of pink. Only Gopal was allowed to stir the kheer because his arm movements were the best coordinated, being used to hard labour.

'You young women have no strength in your waxed arms,' my grandmother would say if smooth-armed women tried to touch the kheer. They were happy to be let off because a slight hesitation in the stirring process would make the milk sulk and fall in a heavy layer at the bottom of the vessel or, worse still, taint the kheer with a faint odour of burnt milk which only my grandmother's sharp nose could pick up at once.

I could not bear to watch them preparing this feast for a trainee priest who, I was sure, had no desire to follow in his father's profession. But when I went to fetch him later that morning, he was ready and dressed for the part. A saffron shawl was draped elegantly around his frail shoulders, making him look older, and his long hair, now worn in smooth, well-oiled curls, added that extra touch of priestliness so desired by my grandmother. His feet, I noticed, were now bare. We sat silently for a while because I did not know how to address him. 'Panditji' would be presumptuous because he had not yet qualified for the job, and 'beta' might be too familiar and probably even blasphemous.

'I have never sat in a Maruti car before,' he said suddenly, leaning forward eagerly. His eyes shone with joy and he looked like a schoolboy dressed up for a play. He told me he was studying in an English medium school and hoped to go to college. 'I have learnt enough Sanskrit to be able to recite the various mantras so that I can carry on my father's work. You see, madam, we get free housing quarters at the temple,' he explained, fiddling with the music system in the car.

When we reached home, I got out of the car, walking ahead of him so that the impact of his small height and underage status would be slightly diffused.

'What is this?—a baby "priestling"!' cried my brother. 'Better get some milk ready, or maybe Farex,' he added, laughing. My young priest heard him but carried on walking up the stairs, his head held high. His eyes took on a cold, steely look which his ancestors must have used to put many a cheeky prince in his proper place. He greeted my grandmother with folded hands but gazed far beyond her shoulders as if already seeing her in the context of the next world. Throughout the shradh ceremony, which he conducted with dignity and skill, he did not smile once. Not when my father tripped over the brass pot as he tried to wash his feet; not when my brother asked him to 'fast forward' the prayers; not even when his dhoti got caught in the new umbrella which was being offered to him. He glanced at all the gifts he would receive at the end of the ceremony with a cool indifference which impressed even my cynical brothers. He just nodded briefly at the collection which consisted of seven brass utensils, a folding bed which my grandmother had bought instead of the charpoy to keep up with the times, three crisp white dhotis, an expensive shawl, a huge black umbrella, a flashy red torch in place of the obligatory lamp, and a massive pile of bedding to last him a lifetime.

Then he sat down to eat. At first he ate slowly, chewing each mouthful thoughtfully. The women watched from the kitchen door, and my grandmother hovered above him like a genie freshly emerged out of the brass lamp. She did not take her eyes off him as he ate, anticipating his needs before he could make even a slight gesture. No words were spoken. Slowly the vegetables vanished, puris disappeared without a trace, yet his plate was never empty, like Krishna's mythical bowl. The women rolled out puris faster and faster and Gopal fried them frantically. The boy priest kept eating at a slow but unwavering pace. My grandmother beamed.

The women took turns to come out and gaze upon him with wonder. Gopal applauded his twenty-fifth puri with the same gleeful cry he kept for Test match victories. Finally, when we, the unbelievers, were getting a bit tense about there being nothing left for us to eat, he stopped with a gentle burp, but not before he had drunk a cauldron of kheer by holding it up to his mouth and finishing it in one breath. My grandmother wept tears of joy.

'You come every year, Panditji,' she whispered.

'Your food is the best I have eaten. Next time, can I bring a few friends? They are not priests, but...,' he hesitated, shedding his earlier haughty stance now that the ceremony was over.

'You bring anyone you want. I will feed your friends and you on this day, as long as I live.'

A year later, my grandmother passed away. The young priest came one last time to pray for her soul and to eat his last meal in our house.

'The food is not the same without her,' he said, but ate non-stop with his usual gusto, to ensure that her journey across the river of death to greater heights was smooth and easy. The shradh ceremony is no longer held by our family and a token amount is given to charity instead. But I know that the boy-priest, who must be middle-aged by now, is still eating his way through life, like a caterpillar, with the benevolent spirit of my grandmother watching over him.

PHULMAKHANI (Lotus Seeds) AND PANEER

250 gms phulmakhani

250 gms tomatoes

250 gms cottage cheese (paneer)

½ tsp coriander powder

½ tsp cumin powder

½ tsp turmeric powder

salt to taste

half a cup plain yogurt

1 tsp oil

Heat oil in a kadai till it is smoking hot. Fry the coriander, cumin and turmeric. Add chopped tomatoes and keep stirring till the oil separates and the mixture is deep red. Put cubes of fresh paneer and half a cup of yogurt, diluted in just enough water to cover the paneer. Add salt and simmer for a few minutes and then add the phulmakhani. Serve while the lotus seeds are crisp and fluffy.

3

Mayadevi's London Yatra

The day Mayadevi turned seventy, seventy-five or eighty (her date of birth was an ever-changing fact depending on her mood), she decided to go to London. Everyone in the family was stunned when she announced this, but no one dared to speak out because the old lady ruled over the entire three-storeyed house with a reign of terror. Whenever she decided to do anything, her three sons and their wives immediately agreed, since they had learnt slowly and bitterly over the years that no one questioned the formidable old lady's whims.

Though there was no need for Mayadevi to give an explanation to her docile and submissive family, she called her sons and gave her reasons for undertaking such a long journey at her age. Mayadevi had never left the house, not even to visit the neighbours, ever since she had come to live here as a fifteen-year-old bride and now she announced she was getting on a plane to go to London to visit her son. 'I want to see Amit before I die,' was all she said. This son of hers had gone to London twenty years ago and never returned to India since then. He wrote to his mother every month. He had tried calling a few times but Mayadevi disliked talking on the phone to anyone and told him not to waste his money. He sent her money often but he did not come to see her.

Amit had an acute phobia of flying. He had somehow endured the flight to London and then decided never to leave the safety of the island. There had been a few short, tension-filled trips to France and to Italy, but these were either by train or by boat. Around every October, as the Pujo season approached, he promised his mother that this year he would get into an aeroplane and come to Calcutta, but his nerve failed him with reassuring regularity each time.

'The wretched boy was always a sissy. He could never cross the road if a cow was standing in the middle. Lizards frightened him and rats made him scream even when he was fifteen years old. I will shame him by going to London—to his very doorstep, even if I have to bathe in the Ganga twenty-one times after I return,' the old lady declared, and the sons and their wives, who thought it a very foolish idea, nodded their heads in agreement as they had done all their lives.

~

Once the momentous decision had been taken, Mayadevi began planning for her journey on a war-like footing. She first applied for a passport and visa, but filled in the forms with a lot of arguments and protests because she did not like the impertinent questions the government dared ask her. Once that ordeal was over, she bought a big register and wrote down her plan of action, step by step.

Then she decided to attack the English language. Though Mayadevi had never been to school, she could read and write Bengali fluently and was far better read than her graduate sons. She could understand simple sentences in English but had never spoken the language to anyone in her entire life since the occasion had never risen. Now she hunted out a tattered old English primer, which belonged to one of her grandchildren, and every morning, after she had finished her puja, folded her Gita away safely and distributed the sanctified sweets, she sat down to study this jam-stained book. The household, usually peaceful and quiet in the mornings, was now filled with Mayadevi's strange rendering of the English primer. Sitting cross-legged on the floor and rocking herself backwards and forwards, she read each line over and over again in a musical singsong as if she were chanting a sacred verse. Then she would suddenly stop and ask herself questions. 'Did Jack fetch the bucket?' she would ask in an accusing tone, and then reply, 'No, Jane fetched the bucket.' She would get up once in a while, adjust her spectacles and take a short walk around the room, holding the closed book near her chest as she had seen her grandson do when he was memorizing a text.

The servants did not dare come near the study area, but watched her nervously from the kitchen doorway. They were sure she was learning English only to terrorize them more effectively. 'At her age she should be only reading the Gita, not repeating jack-jack-jack like a parrot,' they said, but only when within the safety of the servants' quarters. The lesson unnerved the cook so much that he stopped fiddling with the marketing accounts and turned honest, in case the old lady, armed with the English language, caught him out.

The daughters-in-law too found the lessons very odd and giggled quietly in their bedrooms, but they were careful to put on a serious face when they came anywhere near the vicinity of the English lessons. The sons also kept their distance from their mother after their eager efforts to help her with her English pronunciation had met with a cold rebuff. 'For sixty years I have managed this house and my life without any help from you or your late father. I do not have any wish to start now,' she said, dismissing them with a regal wave of the tattered book.

So she carried on learning the primer and the household not only got as used to the strange sounds, but caught the infectious tone too and the servants began humming 'Jack and Jill' as they went about their chores. Within a few weeks, Mayadevi had finished the primer and graduated to more difficult books. She now carried on long conversations with herself to air her newly acquired knowledge of English, and as the days went by, the characters from the primer, the *Teach Yourself English in 21 Days* and other books got mixed up with each other in the most unfortunate, tangled relationships. 'Did Jane go to the grocer's shop alone? No, Mr Smith went too.' 'Mrs Smith is sitting on the bench in the garden with Jack. She is smoking a pipe. How are you, Jack? Quite well, thank you. Where is the tramway?' her voice would drone endlessly till she had learnt all the words in each and every book by heart and so had the rest of the household.

~

Now there were only three months left for the date of departure and Mayadevi went into the next stage of her travel preparations for the great journey which had been named London Yatra by her family, though, of course, behind her back. 'Now I am going to wear shoes,' she announced and ordered one of her sons to get her a pair of black canvas shoes and six pairs of white cotton socks. Mayadevi had always walked barefoot in the house and worn slippers on the rare occasions she went out to inspect the garden. The No. 3 blue rubber slippers lasted her for five years at least, and though they hardly ever stepped on the road, they were washed every day with soap. But in England, these faithful slippers would not do, and so Mayadevi reluctantly and with a martyred air, forced her thin, arthritic feet into her first pair of shoes. For one hour in the morning, after the English lessons, and then another hour after her evening tea, the old lady practised walking in her new shoes. Like an egret stepping out on clumsy, mud-covered feet, the white-clad figure paced up and down the house, accompanied by a rhythmic squeaking of rubber. Soon there were large blisters on her feet, but Mayadevi carried on the struggle like a seasoned warrior and no one heard her expel a single sigh ever. Her sons admired her from a distance, but did not dare to praise her, since they knew she distrusted flattery of any kind and always said, 'Say what you want from me and leave out the butter.' So no one ever praised her, and came straight to the point when asking for favours.

When there was only one month left for the departure, Mayadevi wrote to her son in England and informed him of her plans. He instantly went into a severe panic and telephoned her, which he had rarely done in the last twenty years. 'Ma, please do not undertake such a dangerous journey. Planes are crashing all the time. You can be hijacked to Libya. Air travel is really unsafe now. You wait, I will definitely come home next Pujo,' he screamed hysterically over the bad line.

Mayadevi listened to him patiently and then replied, 'I may be dead by next Pujo. My ticket has been bought. You will come and receive me at the airport and make sure you come alone and not with that giant English wife of yours,' she said and put the phone down firmly though she could hear her son's voice still cackling on the line. From then on, there was total silence from across the ocean, but that did not bother the old lady and she now moved into the final preparations for the London Yatra.

One morning, the old lady called her sons and the family priest for a meeting. The daughters-in-law were not invited, so they took turns to listen at the door. 'In case I die in that foreign land, though God will never do such a thing to me, bring my body back immediately, before they contaminate it. Then see that all the rituals of purification are done properly,' she said, fixing the priest with such an unblinking, fierce look that he began to tremble with fear, thinking that the old lady had died already and was watching him from heaven. Once the plans of how to deal with her dead person had been discussed to her satisfaction, Mayadevi gave them detailed instructions for the purification rites she, if she returned alive, would go through on the very day she came back.

'There is a week-long penance to be done, Brahmins are to be fed and the entire house is to be washed with water from the Ganga. So see that you take leave from office, all of you,' she said to the sons, who understood the importance of the occasion and readily nodded their heads, hoping the meeting had finally ended.

Now only one week was left for the date of departure. A large, battered suitcase, which had been a part of Mayadevi's impressive dowry when she came to this house as a bride, was brought out from the storeroom and Mayadevi began packing. Six white cotton saris, six petticoats and an equal number of blouses, one black sweater and a grey shawl, along with a small, red cloth bag for her Gita and her prayer beads, and a plastic box for her false teeth were the only items she packed. 'Everything, except the Gita and my teeth, will be thrown away when I return, so why waste money?' she said. The suitcase was packed and ready five days in advance and left on top of the stairs like a coveted trophy. Everyone who came or left the house would trip over it, but not a murmur of protest was heard. In fact, the servants proudly dusted it every day and the children approached it with awe.

Then finally, the day of departure arrived. Mayadevi got up before dawn, bathed and went into her prayer room. She knelt before the gods and whispered, 'Give me strength to endure this ordeal and let me not die in that land. I promise to make you new ornaments of gold when I return. Please bring me back safely to you.' She sat for a long time in that small, incense-filled room and only when the first rays of sunlight began to stream in through the windows did she get up and go out to wake up her sons. Soon the entire household was rushing around, though there was nothing very much to do. The suitcase was dusted a few times and the children were made to touch their grandmother's feet every time they passed her way. The sons kept clearing their throats and looking at their watches. 'Has she got everything?' they muttered, but not too loudly, since none of them wanted to go and check. Mayadevi packed five large packets of puffed rice in a cloth bundle and filled up her grandson's plastic water bottle. This was all that Mayadevi going to eat for the next twelve hours, because she was not going to touch any food 'that God knows who had touched.'

The day passed quickly as visitors came to say goodbye. Each one admired the suitcase and, after bumping into it, remarked how light it was. The plane left at 12 o'clock at night, but Mayadevi and her sons were already at the airport four hours before that. They sat solemnly in a row and watched the clock now, instead of their wristwatches. They had never before spent such a concentrated and confined time with their mother and were finding it very difficult to sit so close to her on the plastic chairs.

They took care to change places so that no one had to sit for too long near her and each brother could get some respite. Once in a while, Mayadevi spoke to give some last-minute instructions. Her sons only nodded and cleared their throats once again. At last the flight was announced. The old lady lifted her head and listened carefully. Suddenly one of her sons got carried away by emotion and tried to give his mother a few travel tips, but she got up quietly and joined the long queue of passengers weaving their way to check in. One by one, the sons, bending with difficulty, held back by their middle-age spreads, touched their mother's feet. She blessed them with a rarely seen gentle smile, and as they stood like orphans, she sailed out of their vision and into the gaping door of the security area. The sons were not worried about their aged mother. They only wondered how England would cope.

~

It was raining when the plane landed in London.

A flicker of worry crossed Mayadevi's mind as she wondered whether her still somewhat unsteady shoe-walking ability would be able to manage the wet ground when she went out of the airport. 'It will have to be done,' she said to herself, looking down sternly at the shiny black shoes, as if ordering them to obey her. She adjusted her sari, still crisp and starched after twelve hours, and got ready to leave the plane. Throughout the flight she had sat ramrod straight and when the air hostess had offered to adjust her seat to a more comfortable, reclining position, she had said, 'Why should I sit back like that? I am not ill,' in a sharp voice, freezing the pretty young hostess's smile before it could even begin. She ignored the old lady after that, but could not help glancing nervously at the grey, sari-draped head each time she passed her seat.

Mayadevi's neighbour too had stopped talking to her before they had even crossed the Hindu Kush mountains and now pointedly looked the other way. The English girl had tried to be friendly and helpful and had showed the old lady how to fasten her seatbelt. Mayadevi at first did not say a word and the younger girl thought she was just shy about not being able to speak English and became even friendlier. 'Everyone was so kind to me even though they are so poor. Indians have such large hearts,' she said, warming up to the subject, happily rehearsing what she was going to say to her friends when she reached home, when suddenly Mayadevi opened her mouth for the first time and said, 'Why they not be kind to you? They lick white people's shoes two hundred years and now it become their bad habit like drinking and smoking.' The girl was shocked. Never once, during her travels through the length and breadth of the country, staying only with families, since one could get to know 'real India' that way, and also since hotels were so expensive, had she met with such rudeness. She was gathering her wits to say something sharp in reply, when Mayadevi told her to take her elbow off the armrest. 'I do not want you to touch my sari,' she said. After that they sat silently, a cold wall between them, for the rest of the flight.

When the air hostess came with the meals, Mayadevi shook her head firmly and also crossed her hands over her lap, in the traditional manner of refusing food at Bengali feasts, to doubly confirm her refusal. She then watched the young girl eat her meal and stared at her with an expression of such distaste that the poor girl left her food half-eaten, though she was enjoying the European meal, even a plastic-covered, airline one, after six months of endless dal and chapatis. Once in a while, Mayadevi would eat a handful of puffed rice and take a few sips of water from her plastic bottle. The bundle containing the rice and the water bottle had been carried close to her body throughout the journey, and when the security men at the airport had asked her to send it through the X-ray machine, she had clung to the bundle like a lioness to her cubs and said, 'Touch it and I will throw it in your face. I will starve for the next twelve hours, and if I die, you and your next fourteen generations will have the sin of an old woman's death on your heads.' The security men, trained only to deal with terrorists, did not know how to handle this woman and allowed the old lady and her clumsy bundle to pass without any checking. Actually, Mayadevi did not really need the rice and could easily have stayed without food for many hours at a stretch, since she had been fasting for some auspicious day or the other from the time she was a young girl and her stomach was quite used to stern starvation regimes. But now that the plane was about to land, it suddenly gave a loud rumble of protest, startling Mayadevi by this uncharacteristic rebellion.

The young girl heard it too and allowed herself a small, mean smile. 'Old grumbling cow, hope she has a bad time here,' she thought, but then immediately felt guilty and filled up Mayadevi's landing form for her. Mayadevi never even said a 'thank you', and as soon as the plane came to a halt, she shot up from her seat. She marched down the aisle, clutching her food bundle close to her body so that no one could contaminate it by touching it and was the first passenger to get out of the aircraft. She then slowed down and attached herself to a group of Indian passengers who had also just come off the plane. She followed them closely, but when they reached the immigration area and began queuing up, she walked past them and planted herself firmly at the head of the line. No one could ask an old lady to move back, and even if someone had, Mayadevi had her steely look ready. The man at the immigration counter smiled at her kindly, even though it was against his principles to smile at immigrants or visitors of any hue. In return for the rare grin, he received the famous dead-fish stare, under which innumerable men and women of Calcutta, young and old, had quailed. The young official felt sheepish for no reason at all and quickly called for an interpreter, an almost SOS urgency creeping into his voice. 'I speak English. You know English. You speak English with me,' Mayadevi said clearly.

The immigration official cleared his throat and said, 'How long do you plan to stay in the UK?' and when Mayadevi said nothing, he repeated the question, adding a 'Madam' this time.

'No need to say again and again. I answer you. I stay in this land one week only. Not a day longer. You can tell your Queen,' said Mayadevi.

The stunned official stamped her passport with a resounding thump and waved her on as fast as he could. 'This is one old bird who is not lying to me. Won't ever catch her working in Selfridges, for sure,' he said to his colleague with a nervous laugh, as if some ordeal had been passed.

Mayadevi again followed the passengers she had marked out earlier and made sure they collected her suitcase and carried it for her in a trolley. Her son was waiting for her outside when she finally emerged, but even though she saw him at once, she gave no sign that she recognized him.

The sixty-year-old, extremely successful dentist, member of the Royal College of Dentists, did not dare raise his arm and wave to his mother. She walked towards him slowly, and after she reached him, stood staring at him as if he were a total stranger. The son lurched forward and made an awkward, half-bending movement to touch his mother's feet, but at the same time surreptitiously tried to look as if he was tying his shoelaces. Mayadevi, who was on full alert, her eyes carefully scrutinizing her son for faults, pounced like an eagle on the first wrong move. 'Ashamed to touch your mother's feet now, are you? A mother who has not long to live, but even then has travelled such a great distance, fasting for twelve hours, sitting with all kinds of half-castes so that she can see her son,' she hissed. Amit, who was well known in the dentists' circles for his dry, sharp wit, was about to defend himself with a few crisp, well-chosen words, but before he could speak, something clicked inside him. As he looked into that old lined face, an irrational fear rose in his heart, jolting his memory and he said in a whining, childish voice, 'No, Ma…I…so many people here,' he stammered helplessly and then folded his hands and bowed.

Once she had established the old family hierarchy and satisfied at her son's obedience, Mayadevi told him to pick up her suitcase and take her to his home. Though the mother and son had not seen each other for forty years, they drove to his semi-detached house in the tree-lined suburbs in unbroken, stony silence. The mother asked no questions and the son offered no explanations, because he somehow felt that she knew everything about him already and disapproved strongly. When they reached home, Mayadevi got out of the car in a suspicious, stealthy manner as if she was expecting hidden traps in the neatly laid out garden. Mother and son entered the house like two mourners returning from a funeral, and when his wife came out of the kitchen to greet them, Amit almost burst into tears with relief.

'Welcome to England, Mrs Banerjee. Hope you had a nice flight,' Martha, Amit's wife, said cheerfully. Mayadevi looked up at her tall daughter-in-law through the top of her spectacles for a few long, uncomfortable, silent seconds and then said, 'I want to wash hands. Everything so dirty.' Martha's good-natured face showed a brief flicker of surprise, but she beamed at her mother-in-law and said, 'Come and see your room and then we will have a nice cup of tea. Hope you like the new curtains we put up for you. Amit did not know what your favourite colour was, so I chose blue,' she prattled on, her voice full of genuine affection for the old lady she had never met before. Amit crept up to shelter behind his wife's ample frame as his mother examined the room, and cringed each time Martha went too close to her. He knew what would happen if Martha touched her by mistake. 'Are you feeling cold? Shall I turn up the central heating?' asked Martha, suddenly feeling the cold herself. Though Mayadevi was shivering in her thin cotton sari, she said, 'Not cold, only wash hands, so much dirty!' Martha quickly led her to the bathroom, gaily decorated with trailing, plastic plants and fluffy rugs. Mayadevi slammed the door shut on Martha's smiling face and began to wash her hands.

First she washed the taps thoroughly and then she began rinsing the soap, though it was a brand new one. Then she finally washed her hands meticulously four times in a row. When she had finished, she turned the tap off with her elbow, so as not to touch the tap with her freshly washed hands again. She dried her hands by shaking them about in the air, looking scornfully, as she did so, at the flowered hand towels Martha had put out for her. Then she went out to look for her son. 'How will I bathe in that jungle with plants you call bathroom? Why has she put carpets in the bathroom? To hide the dirty floor?' she charged with full force, pleased to have found something to complain about so quickly.

'Ma, please…she will hear you,' said Amit, glancing nervously at the kitchen door, even though they were speaking in Bengali. 'You must be tired. Why don't you eat the rice I have made for you and go to sleep now?' he said, desperately hoping she would agree. Surprisingly, she did. 'If you are telling the truth that she did not make it. I will not eat it then,' was the only half-hearted resistance she put up and followed him to the kitchen. 'I cooked it, Ma. She did not even touch it. I am not lying to you,' he said and flushed when he saw Martha watching him, even though he knew she could not understand what he had said. But Mayadevi made sure that the message had got through by giving her a triumphant look. She took out her false teeth with a sharp, satisfied click and sat down to eat. The meal, a bowl of overcooked rice and a muddy brown dal, was consumed quickly and noisily as Mayadevi chewed with her gums, and when she had finished, she took her plate to the sink and washed it carefully twice. She shook it dry by waving it in the air and then kept it as far away as possible from the other plates and dishes. Martha's friendly smile had by now faded to a bewildered, confused look and she stood silently, watching the water from the plate drip all over her hospital-like, sparkling-clean kitchen floor. But she did not know what to do or say. Amit stood next to her, wearing the expression of a sad, unhappy man, expecting even worse times ahead.

Mayadevi, quite content now with the way things had gone so far, left them both and went to her room. She dragged the bedcover off the bed, spread it on the floor, and then, after saying her prayers, fell fast asleep at once. She woke up in the middle of the night and sat bolt upright. The greyish-yellow street light streamed in through the window and the sky outside was a lighter shade than she had ever seen. Calcutta seemed very far away.

'God forgive me for crossing the black waters, I will return home soon,' said Mayadevi, feeling lonely for the first time in her long, solitary life.

~

The next day passed very much like the first one, only Mayadevi cooked the food for herself and Amit. He felt guilty about not eating with Martha but his mother's contemptuous, 'Ha! A slave to his flour-coloured wife,' plus the delicious fragrance of long-forgotten, favourite dishes, compelled him to sit down and eat with his mother every evening as soon as he came back from work. Martha never complained and he did not dare to ask her what they both did during the day, but he got the answer anyway, judging by the new, unhappy lines on his wife's forever-cheerful face.

Like two boxing champions trapped in a ring, Martha and Mayadevi circled around the house, avoiding each other but at the same time keeping a wary eye on what the other person was doing. The old lady would listen as her daughter-in-law went about doing her housework and then she would tiptoe out, her eyes gleaming like a fault-finding laser beam, to check out the house. She opened drawers, peered under the beds and ran her fingers over the windowpanes. But she could not find any dust or cobwebs, as she did on her weekly checking rounds in her house in Calcutta. Angry and bored, Mayadevi took to sitting in her bedroom in sullen silence for the entire day. Martha did try from time to time to make a few friendly overtures to the old lady, but each time she met a solid wall of silent rebuff. Mayadevi would shut her eyes tightly and pretend to chant her prayers every time her daughter-in-law looked into her room. She never wanted to go out to look at the shops, watch television or drink tea, and Martha could not think of anything else to cajole the old lady out of the room.

Slowly the six days of unspoken tension passed, and Mayadevi happily began packing her bag once more. 'Thank God, it is over, the wretched trip,' she muttered. The last day of the visit was a Saturday, and Amit had taken the day off from his clinic. He had been hoping that some emergency would crop up and he would have to rush to the clinic, but he knew very well that it was a foolish thought and a dentist very rarely had a crisis of broken molars or sudden cavities in his career. He decided to bravely face the situation and take his mother out shopping. Martha, her good-natured spirit still alive, offered to come along too, but Amit said in a sad voice, 'No, you rest, dear. I will take her…alone'. as if he was going off to slay some dreaded dragon. But Martha insisted on coming along to give him unspoken support. They drove to the large shopping centre nearby, Mayadevi sitting at the back, spurning all friendly remarks and efforts at showing her the sights of London. When they reached the huge, glittering building, there was an embarrassing tussle in the car park. Mayadevi did not want to get out from the car.

'Why should I go to this big shop? What do I want to buy from here?' she asked her son, facing him squarely. Amit stared helplessly at the giant shopping complex with ten floors of the world's best merchandise, but he could not think of a single thing his mother could buy there. 'Well, now that we are here, let us go in. You can tell everyone at home what you saw, can't you?' he said with a wide, foolish grin, as if he was talking to a child. Mayadevi snorted in the haughty, dignified way only she could. But now that she had made her protest, she stepped briskly out of the car. They went into the building, and after a slight pause to fight the escalator, where Mayadevi's sari got stuck in the gap between the steps and she, thinking Amit had stepped on it, kept scolding loudly, they disentangled her and entered the fairyland of gifts, cosmetics, and the perfume and lingerie department.

Mayadevi suddenly stood still. She felt as if she had been struck by lightning. In her entire seventy-five-odd years, she had never seen a world like this. Hundreds of bright lights gleamed everywhere she looked. Dazzling, blinding mirrors as tall as trees, and walls that had solid gold lamps on them. There were countless mysterious, colourful objects she could not recognize, on every glossy surface. Silken bits of lace were draped all over glass shelves and though they had an odd shape like two cups, Mayadevi, who had never worn any undergarments like most other women of her age, thought they were the most beautiful lace decorations. She could smell the fragrance drifting up from the glittering glass bottles filled with magical potions. It was the most powerful and sweet incense she had ever smelt.

There were jewels as big as eggs in boxes that shone with silver and gold threads. Mayadevi felt that she had died and come to heaven, only the people wrong. 'There should have been our gods and goddesses in this paradise, not these pale humans,' she said softly to herself, not moving in case it was a dream. Her daughter-in-law suddenly understood what had happened to the old lady. She took her arm and gently guided her through the maze-like, narrow lanes of the department store, overflowing with gleaming, expensive merchandise. For once Mayadevi did not flinch at her touch and followed Martha meekly as if she was a celestial maiden guiding her in paradise.

'I think we should get her a nice warm jumper, Amit,' Martha said to her husband, who had not yet noticed the sudden change in his mother. They went to the women's department and Martha picked up a pale-blue cardigan. 'No, no, only white,' whispered Mayadevi, still in a trance. Martha found a fluffy white one quickly and also a soft, lacy white shawl to go with it. She presented them both to the old lady with a friendly smile. But this gift was a greater shock for Mayadevi than seeing the big department store, in all its glory, for the first time. Her late husband, her many children and countless relatives had never given her a present. Her steely old eyes, unused to crying, filled with tears and she took Martha's hand and shook it as she had seen people in her English phrase book do. 'Good girl, very well, thank you,' she said to her daughter-in-law, showering her with all the polite words she knew in English.

By the time they reached home, Mayadevi's brief moment of weakness had passed and her vision had cleared. She was her old self again, but there was a certain change in her demeanour. She did not actually smile, but her eyes had lost that cold look and she called Martha by her name. The next day, before she left for the airport, she let Martha make her a cup of tea, and muttered quick thanks. As Amit watched his mother drink the tea, he wondered if Martha would ever realize what a sacrifice and effort it meant for the old lady to cast off age-old taboos and accept this cup of tea made by her foreign daughter-in-law. The journey to the airport was silent this time too, but not an unhappy, uncomfortable one. When the time came for Mayadevi to leave, she patted Martha's hand and said, 'When I die, you come to Calcutta for my funeral. Let my fool of a son be. You come.' Then, after making sure that her son had touched her feet properly, she walked into the 'Passengers only' area. She did not turn around to wave at them, though she knew she would probably never see her son again. She was content that she had done her duty and now she looked forward to the year-long penance, purifications and sacrificial rituals she would have to do to wash away the sins of the London Yatra.

4

Anadi's Journey

In the drowsy heat of the afternoon, the pond lay still and only the shadows of the coconut palms danced on its surface. The air smelt warm and damp as if it was going to rain. Anadi gathered the bundle of wet clothes which his sister had just washed and carried them to a patch of sunlight which fell in a jagged circle near the pond. He lay them out one by one, chasing away the butterfly that swarmed around his head. His mother had told him that if a butterfly ever sat on his right shoulder, he would never get married and even at the age of ten Anadi longed to be a householder. He wanted a big house, a pretty wife and tall sons. But the house would not be a thatched one like his village home, which swayed and moaned during the monsoon rains. It would be built with red bricks, held firmly together with cement, have painted walls and a high iron gate and it would not be in Bishtupur, but somewhere far away in a shimmering city which Anadi was not certain existed outside his imagination.

Anadi's father had died when he was six months old and his mother, too sick and frail to look after this child of late middle age, had given him to her eldest daughter who had no children of her own. Anadi spread the clothes out to dry and then sat down in the shade of the mango tree to read the new book his brother had sent him from Calcutta. Books were not easy to find in this small village of Bishtupur, which was a five-hour boat journey from the nearest town. It took two days by boat steamer, train, and then finally by bus to reach Calcutta, a city which seemed to Anadi as awesome and unattainable as paradise.

Anadi went every evening to watch the boat arrive at the river bank, which was just a few minutes away from his house, behind a grove of banana trees. He sat under a tree, a little away from the crowded jetty, and watched the passengers as they came off the boat, carefully looking for any signs that would tell him something about the city they had just visited. But the men looked as ordinary as they had done when they had left Bishtupur. Their faces did not wear new expressions nor were they surrounded by shining auras, which a visit to the city should surely have marked them with. The journey they had undertaken, so full of mystery, danger and excitement, did not seem to have changed them in any way. Anadi often followed them home, listening to their conversations, but their voices sounded the same and they still talked about their debts, about the rice crop, and the recent haul of fish as they did when they sat in their courtyards in the village. These men had been to Calcutta—the very name made Anadi breathless with joy and fear—they had sat in a train, seen motor cars, heard their blaring horns, walked down streets lit by gas lights and heard the radio and yet they remained unchanged, still talking like ordinary men of debts, rice and fish.

Anadi felt his ten years a heavy burden which clung to his shoulders, never allowing him to be free. And it was not just him, everyone in the village remained weighed down, standing still in one place, as if afraid to move. The old men sat in a shaded corner of the courtyard, their gnarled hands always holding the stem of the hookah in the same position. The children played the same games over and over near the pond, their bodies thin and agile forever. Their mothers too always wore the same expressions as they quarrelled and laughed amongst themselves. His house, surrounded by evergreen banana and coconut trees, remained unchanged in every season and, day after day, his mother sat in the same dark corner of the kitchen, cleaning an endless quantity of rice.

Anadi knew that another world existed somewhere far away on the other side of the river, but he could never reach it because Bishtupur would never let him go. Each day he watched the boat leave Bishtupur without him, feeling as helpless as Kanu, the blind boy who could not walk to the pond though he knew it was there.

'Let the boy stay at home now and help you. He is old enough,' his mother said, her voice faint with fever, 'schools and studies will only make him grow wings and fly away to Calcutta.' Anadi sat near her bed, hoping that if he did not make a noise they would forget about taking him away from school. 'No, Ma, he is a very bright boy and studies hard. Not like the other boys in the school. This one will go far, maybe even to an English college in Calcutta. Let him finish his matriculation and try for a scholarship,' his brother-in-law said. Anadi suddenly felt free, as if all his fears had floated away out of the window above his mother's bed and, no longer afraid to be seen, he ran out of the house. It seemed to him that the entire village had changed and the people, the houses, the trees all swirled around him and even the pond was no longer stagnant and still, but rippled with new shades of green.

The boat rocked on the edge of the bank, its ropes straining as the passengers pushed their way forward to find a place. As the boat moved away, Bishtupur became smaller and smaller and then finally disappeared. Anadi felt it had merged into the world waiting for him across the river and he knew he was not leaving, but only forming a bridge between his childhood and adult life.

~

The dolphins jumped out of the water, forming an arc over the waves and then disappeared into the sea. Anadi waited for them to appear again but they seemed to have vanished deep into some secret hiding place beneath the ocean. The ship moved in a wavy, uneven line cutting through the grey blue waters like a blunt knife. Anadi wondered if the river in Bishtupur had also merged into this vast ocean. He leaned over the railing as if he could see traces of the muddy river in the ocean and then he laughed at his own foolishness.

'Not seasick any more, boy?' asked an elderly Bengali gentleman as he strolled past. He wore a white suit with a big hat and carried a cane which he kept tapping on the deck like a blind man. 'I tell everyone it is the boiled cabbage on the ship that makes people sick, not the sea. Though we have been away from Calcutta only for a week, I already miss my mother's cooking. Mustard fish and banana flower curry…coconut prawns…Oh! Ma!' he sighed as he looked far into the ocean as if waiting for his mother to suddenly emerge from the sea. Anadi was surprised that such an old man still had a mother who was alive. She must be ninety at least. 'My mother is a hundred and one years old and still supervises the cooking at home. My wife is terrified of her,' said the old man, suddenly breaking into English. 'Must practise your English, young man. Practice makes your English perfect. Every morning, while brushing your teeth, recite to yourself all the difficult verbs, especially the present continuous tense, which we Bengalis find so difficult,' he said and began to mutter, 'have been eating, have been bathing, have been sick....' Then he walked away, tapping his cane in rhythm to his repeated sentences.

Anadi wished he had stayed back to talk to him. He seemed like a well-travelled man and would know everything about England. It was lonely on this huge ship which was as big as all of Bishtupur and had more people in it. Anadi could not stop comparing his village to every new thing he saw. Calcutta, frightening with its endless streams of people and black clouds of smoke had seemed to him like a monster raging in a storm. This was not the city of his dreams. But he spent three happy years in the Scottish Church College where he had got a scholarship to study after his matriculation from the village school. He remembered how the entire village had come to the river bank to see him off and his mother too had come out of the house for the first time in his life. She seemed much younger in daylight, almost like a stranger. 'Bathe every day and do not eat beef,' she had whispered to him and then left without looking back. Her face appeared before him now and he felt like crying out 'Ma...' like the old man had done. He knew he would see her again when he returned home because she would never leave her dark corner in the kitchen.

~

The dishes swayed gently on the table and Anadi hesitated though everyone else had already begun to eat. 'Is it beef?' he whispered to the old gentleman who was sitting next to him. 'No, it is veal, delicious, but put some pepper on it first.' Relieved because the aroma from the steaming dish was making his mouth water, Anadi quickly began to eat.

'I had to throw my sacred thread into the river after that. How could I explain to my mother that veal was not related to seal?' he said as the laughter died down. His German was quite fluent now, in fact much better than his English which held traces of his village accent. In London, the other Indians had often made fun of his English and he remembered his first day at the Royal College of Mines. 'Just arrived from the paddy fields?' a tall young man asked him in Bengali, mimicking his village dialect. 'Yes, do you know my village—Bishtupur?' Anadi asked eagerly. 'No, my friend, I don't. But I can smell the mustard oil and recognize those Kahnai-tailor clothes from far,' he replied in English as the group of boys cackled with laughter. England was freezing cold with grey skies and greyer buildings. It never stopped raining. This was not his village rain which raged through in a brief flash of temper, washing the trees clean and making the coconuts and mangoes drop into their courtyard. It was not the frightening monsoon which created havoc, but then receded to leave the land fertile and green. The rain here was like the continuous weeping of an old woman to whose sorrow everyone had become indifferent. People did not stay indoors when it rained, watching it fearfully from their windows as he had done, they put on their raincoats, opened their umbrellas and walked about as if it was normal weather.

Anadi was happy to leave England and sad too because he had made friends with a few English boys. But the last four months had erased the picture of a glorious, golden land, which he had read about and admired all through school and college. This was not the England of his dreams and these timid, grey men, always clutching umbrellas, were not the mighty rulers of his country but imposters who had somehow taken over England.

Calcutta, London…both the cities had let him down like old, trusted friends who had turned into enemies. But Frieburg, a small town in Germany that he never knew of previously and had no expectations from, was perfect. Anadi liked the unhurried, friendly pace of the town and its crowd of young students. Old men sat in sunlit parks and children played familiar games on the empty streets. In 1931, Germany was brimming with overconfidence, which infected the youth and filled them with a sense of their own importance.

'Anadi, you must eat well or you will become thin and then what will your mother say?' said Mutti as she placed a huge plate of meat and potatoes in front of him. Knowing well that his mother would rather he starve than eat beef, Anadi quickly began to eat before the muttering of his mother's voice in his head became too loud. Mutti, his landlady, had adopted him from the first day he appeared on her doorstep, lean and hungry, unable to speak a word of German. He looked at her kind face and wondered if she had been his mother in another life.

When he received his Doctorate in Engineering, she was the one who celebrated with a huge cake and tears of joy while his own relatives in Calcutta were somewhat bewildered. 'You went to become an engineer but now you say you are a doctor?' they asked.

The day he left Germany, Anadi heard Hitler's voice on the radio and as the words raged in anger, he suddenly knew that the world he was leaving would never be the same again.

~

'The girl is very pretty but she has lived in Delhi most of her life. Hope she is not too smart,' his uncle said. Anadi nodded vaguely, too nervous to speak. 'The girl's father is a government officer, plays tennis with the British, but luckily, her mother is very orthodox. So shake hands with the father and touch the mother's feet.'

Anadi, overcome by stage fright, did exactly the opposite much to everyone's amazement. 'He has just come from Germany,' said his uncle and the relatives, assembled to inspect him, seemed satisfied with this explanation. Since the father was 'modern', he was allowed to see the girl. But her face was a hazy blur and all that he could remember was she was very short and had thick wavy hair. 'Wasn't she slightly plump?' he asked his aunt, hoping she would describe her. 'It is good to be plump. Some clever mothers make their daughters wear two or three petticoats to make them look nice and plump,' said his aunt, who was pleased with the match.

After fifty years and four children, Meera was as plump as ever with a thick mane of gleaming black hair. Anadi was terrified of his wife whose diminutive size packed a fiery temper which flared up at the oddest of things, but remained calm in the face of danger. Though just nineteen, she had travelled with him to the lonely towns in remote areas where his work as an engineer took him. In Giridi, they had lived in a huge, dilapidated bungalow, which was haunted and Meera read *The Canterville Ghost* aloud every evening, hoping to lure the resident ghost. In Bhilai, she had turned a snake-filled pit into a lovely garden and when he landed the car on the verandah during his first and last attempt at driving, she had just laughed. In Burnpur, she taught herself the correct English etiquette to deal with the haughty British ladies. Mutti had taught him how to eat with a fork and knife, but he still got confused sometimes and had once tried to cut through a layer of spaghetti as it streamed down his chin. The entire restaurant had applauded him when he finally succeeded with one final slash and cut off the spaghetti like an expert barber chopping off a full-grown beard.

Meera and he had lived in so many different homes, in so many cities, yet he remembered the name and number on each gate, the colour of the curtains, the trees in the garden, the names of their neighbours and the dogs they had had. 'This is a Burnpur story,' he would say. 'No, it's a Bhilai one, it has Honey and Sarala in it…,' his children would argue, when he reminisced. His children, of whom he was so proud, were very different from him and he wondered what they would say if ever he took them back to Bishtupur. Would his son, a brilliant student at the medical college, sit under the mango tree and read through the day as he had done? His daughters, so smart and knowledgeable about everything in the world, who had already travelled to various parts of the world at an age when he had never set eyes on a bicycle, would they walk to the pond to collect mangoes after a storm?

Bishtupur was so far now, much further than the outside world had been when he stood by the river, waiting. It was in another country now and his village existed only in his memory and yet it was closer and more real to him than ever before.

~

Anadi put his book down on the table and looked out of the window. A strange sound, which he had heard half a century ago, suddenly floated up to him. He opened the door and went out. An old man stood at the gate carrying a basket full of small paper packets. 'Sahib, you want coconut sweets?' he asked in broken Hindi. 'Are you from Khulna district?' Anadi asked, his tongue savouring the dialect after so many years. 'Yes…yes…Dada,' the man replied, happy to speak in his own language in this strange city. They both began talking at once. Coconut palms swayed above him and the pond rippled in the sun. Anadi could smell the wet earth by the river and he heard the village women call out to their children in shrill voices.

When the youngest daughter came home from college, she found her father sitting on the floor of the drawing room with a strange, bedraggled man in a white dhoti. Sounds of laughter filled the house and they spoke in a strange language which sounded familiar, but she could not understand a word. Her father's voice had lost its firm deep tone and he now talked in an excited, high-pitched, almost childish voice.

Anadi saw his daughter watching him from the door but did not call her in. What could she have to say to this old man from a village near Khulna? He was as alien to her as she was to him and only Anadi could link them together. This stranger who sold coconut sweets and jaggery from door to door understood him more than his beloved daughter.

'Tell me, did you have a deaf teacher in your school called Kanai?'

'Yes, and a headmaster who gave us a holiday every second day because he wanted to sleep.'

'Do you remember the fish that swam into the paddy fields after the rains and the way the coconuts fell on our heads during a storm?'

Together, they were in their village once more. It was as if he had left his beloved family, this house built with bricks and cement in a city he admired, and slowly erasing the decades of journeys, years of adapting to the unfamiliar, he had now gone home to Bishtupur.

5

Trials of a Tall Aunt

Roopbala's pilgrimage to Badrinath at the young age of thirty-four was planned by the gods long before she came into this world. It all started when the genes of some Amazonian ancestor, lying dormant for ages, were suddenly activated in her, making her 5 ft 10 in tall. An unusual, but not extraordinary height for a woman, but it sat upon her like a deformity and ruined her life because her husband, only 5 ft 4 in, hated her from the day he set eyes on her. It was not that she was hideously ugly or undesirable in any way to merit such an instantaneous hatred from him at first sight. In fact, she was quite pleasant to look at, with delicate features, large doe-like eyes and gleaming black tresses which reached down to her knees. Her only fault, an unforgivable one in her husband's eyes, was that she stood a clear six inches taller than him. If she had been just an inch or two above his head, then things might not have been so bad. He could have told her not to stand next to him and also taught her to stoop a little when they walked together and their married life might have been different and Roopbala would have gone for a pilgrimage to Badrinath after leading a full life, at the proper age of seventy or above. But those six extra, hateful inches which made her tower above her husband, shattering his fragile ego, altered everything in Roopbala's life.

Her husband Gajanath's heart raged with anger and humiliation every time he had to lift his head to look up at her. He was sure the villagers sniggered behind their backs, and once he even heard a child in the street laugh and say, 'Look, the husband is so short and the wife like a palm tree,' but when he turned around to strangle the boy there and then, there was no one. Gajanath blamed his parents for this tragedy that had ruined his standing in society and made him an object of ridicule. How could he, the biggest landowner's one and only son, a matriculate, walk out in public with this giant of a woman trailing behind him, casting her evil shadow on his head and making him look shorter than he already was? The parents knew how unhappy their beloved son was, but they were helpless to do anything now. They had married him off to Roopbala at a very young age, when the girl had been quite dainty and petite, showing no signs of the Amazon she would grow up to be in the future. She was the only daughter of a very wealthy father and they were keen to clinch the match early, before some other party grabbed her.

Child marriage had been banned by the British government recently, but what did they know about the problems of finding girls with a good dowry for a boy who was, to put it kindly, not exactly a beauty. In fact, they said in the village that his mother had been frightened by a bull just before she gave birth to him and the dire effects of that experience showed clearly on the child's face and temperament from a very early age. Gajanath was dark-skinned, goggle-eyed and his face was set solidly on his stocky body with almost no sign of a neck. His lower jaw always jutted a few inches out, as if ready for combat any time. His temper flared up as suddenly as a matchstick on dry grass and his touchiness was famous in the village. No one dared to even greet him in case they said something to annoy him. They remembered how once a newcomer had made an innocent, passing remark about how the mustard had flowered so well even though it was still so short and the boy had charged headlong into the man, thrown him to the ground and bitten him on his arm. The man had left the village never to come back, but the boy had waited for him with an axe for one week.

The family knew there would be trouble when they went to fetch Roopbala from her parent's house after she had reached the age of puberty. They stared aghast when she gambolled into the room as tall and elegant as a giraffe, even wondering for a brief moment if the girl had been changed, but then they remembered she was their only daughter. They kept their shock and horror well hidden, recalling the huge amount of money that had been given at the time of marriage, which had been spent already many years ago, and quickly patted the towering girl on the shoulder, since they could not reach her head. They took her back with them to the village reluctantly, and as soon as they reached home, Gajanath, who had stayed back, threw such a dramatic and shattering fit that the entire village ran out to watch him. He ranted and raved, his short body shook with spasms and he rolled his eyes till only the whites showed. He foamed at the mouth and bit anyone who tried to come near him. In fact, he looked so much like a bull at this moment that an actual bull, grazing nearby, bellowed in joyful recognition. But nothing could be done now, so the father quickly hid the bride from his son and hoped things would settle down. But five years had passed since she had entered their old house, banging her forehead on the low doorway, and Roopbala's husband still hated her with the same passion. In fact, his hatred for her grew stronger every day, the flames being fanned by the fact that Roopbala seemed to be growing taller. Everyone told him this could not be possible, because she was now twenty-one years old, but Gajanath could see her adding on inches before his eyes. He took care never to stand next to her or walk with her anywhere. Her very presence made this short, stocky thirty-two-year-old man break into a rage which was so strong that it covered him with a deep red flush and made the veins on his forehead stand out. The bull began to look benign and kindly compared to him now.

Gajanath had not spoken to his wife even once in the last five years and had never touched her. She did not understand why she repulsed him so much and tried her best to earn his affection. She learnt to cook his favourite dishes from his mother, washed his clothes, swept and cleaned his room herself, and was always alert to his movements in the house, in case he needed something, but even then all she got for her efforts was a low, angry growl or a glare from his rolling eyes each time he saw her.

Soon she realized that the only way to make him happy was to keep out of his sight, so she began hiding each time she heard his footsteps. But she still continued to look after him, constantly alert to his every demand, yet remaining unseen. It was a lonely, sad life for her in the old house and Roopbala often wondered why. She spent her time reading religious books, praying and stitching clothes for all the needy children of the village. Her mother-in-law treated her with contempt too, but since she was afraid of her husband, who was fond of Roopbala, she did not dare say anything openly. But she muttered constantly under her breath. 'God knows what they fed her at home to make her into a mountain. It is shameless for a woman to be so tall,' she would say to all the visitors and

Roopbala merged further into the shadows to hide herself. The years passed slowly, filled with a never-ending, heavy gloom. Her father-in-law, who had always been kind to her and protected her from the son, passed away, and just a few months after that her mother-in-law too died, lamenting to the last that she had seen no grandchild.

Now Roopbala and Gajanath were alone in the huge, empty house. They lived in an oasis of oppressive silence, while around them trees flowered, birds sang continuously in joyful notes and the village children played noisy, cheerful games just outside their doorstep. Roopbala often watched them from the window but dared not go out to the village, because her husband hated her appearing in public. But Gajanath himself often went out at night and stayed away till early morning and Roopbala was left alone in the stifling, dark house. There had been a few old servants, but they too left one by one, unable to bear the depressing atmosphere that had now taken over the entire house. 'They are like two ghosts walking around. Chhoto babu does not see her, but hates even her shadow. Boudi just sits quietly all day. I feel scared with them. Give me a good, nagging housewife any day; at least they are real flesh and blood,' said the last old maidservant after she had packed up and left.

Roopbala now did all the work by herself, and one day, when she was reaching out to pick up a jar from the highest shelf, Gajanath decided to murder her. The sight of her long arm, easily picking up things from places where he could reach only by standing on a stool, drove him blind with rage and his crazed mind began weaving schemes to get rid of this witch his parents had saddled him with. He had started drinking heavily ever since his father had died, and his eyes, bloodshot to begin with, were now two deep-crimson pools. He seemed to have shrunk with age while his once-lissome wife had grown quite heavy and now stood not only taller but more solidly built than him. 'Had she been a normal-sized woman, I could have easily strangled her. But this mountain, how will I get rid of this mountain?' he thought, trembling with anger. 'How much poison will she need for that body?' he thought with disgust. Then, as he was going to lift his glass to his lips, he suddenly saw his father's shotgun hanging on the wall. His father had kept this loaded gun ever since a thief had crept into the house and stolen the silver spittoon from right under his bed as he slept. 'I will shoot her, the elephant,' he thought excitedly and almost spilt his glass of country liquor. 'I will shoot her with my father's gun. He brought this monster home for me, his gun can get rid of her now.'

Roopbala went about doing her chores in the kitchen, unaware of the plot of her imminent murder. Like every night, she served the food in a plate, and after leaving it outside his room, she ate and went to sleep. Gajanath waited till the moon was high up in the sky and then he put his glass down and walked unsteadily to the wall where the gun was hanging. He stretched out his arm to take if off the nail, but the gun was hanging far above his reach. Cursing loudly, he picked up a chair and dragged it to the wall. 'Everything has been made for giants in this house,' he muttered and climbed on the chair, his legs shaking. Just as his fingers had closed on the butt of the gun, the leg of the rickety old chair collapsed under him and he fell with a thundering crash. The entire empty and silent house echoed his downfall, magnifying it tenfold, and Roopbala came running into the room. 'What is it? What happened?' she said, taking care to stay out of sight. Gajanath lay sprawled on the floor, sweat pouring down his flushed face that he wiped angrily with his hand. Then he picked up the gun which had fallen to the floor with him. 'I am going to kill you, you shameless, tall, witch of a woman,' he slurred as he tried to get up. Roopbala moved back alarmed. Gajanath took two faltering steps forward.

'Don't. Please don't. I have never harmed you. Don't kill me,' she said.

'You have humiliated me, made me a figure of mockery,' shouted Gajanath and tried desperately to focus his glazed eyes on his victim.

Roopbala, adept at hiding herself from her husband's wrathful eyes, disappeared into the shadows at once. This angered him even more and he lurched forward blindly. Suddenly his foot caught the leg of the chair and he tripped over. The gun flew out of his hands and landed at Roopbala's feet. She stood staring at it in horror, and then, her instincts, inherited probably from the same Amazonian ancestor who had given her height, began to work. She leapt forward and grabbed the gun. 'You move back…or I… will shoot you,' she said, amazed at how loudly she spoke. 'Go back,' she repeated and added, 'Please, I beg you….'

He was her husband, after all, and she was not going to kill him. Gajanath's eyes now bulged out of their sockets madly and he roared like a wounded, trapped tiger. He kicked at the chair to move it out of his way, but his strength was so ferocious and his aim so crooked that he drove the chair into the door and at the same time brought the curtain rod down. Roopbala didn't know what to do now. Her husband lay struggling under the heavy folds of a velvet curtain. She could hear his threats spoken in a choked, muffled voice as he tried to extricate himself. Then suddenly he stood up and lunged at her, still entangled in the velvet curtain, just his two eyes exposed where the curtain rings would have been. Roopbala held out the gun in front of her like a shield and Gajanath, thinking it was her arm, pulled at it with all his might. The explosion shook the entire house and Roopbala hid her head in her hands. Paralysed with fear, she stood absolutely still. Then she opened her eyes and saw blood oozing out from under the curtain and she knew she had shot her husband dead. No sound came from the velvet bundle and Roopbala did not dare to touch it.

All she could think of was running away from this blood-soaked velvet heap which was her late husband. Roopbala forced herself to think clearly. She knew she had to get away before it was daylight. Even now someone could have heard the shot and might come in to inspect. She ran into her room, quickly packed a few clothes, snatched up the bag of her jewellery she kept hidden under her bed, and after folding her hands to the garlanded pictures of gods, her late parents and her in-laws, Roopbala fled into the dark night. She walked all night, taking care to creep through the standing crops of wheat till she had left the village boundaries behind. Now there was no danger of meeting any villager who would instantly recognize her as the landowner's wife.

Just as the sky was getting lighter, she managed to catch a bullock cart which would take her to the nearest town. Luckily, Roopbala had some money tucked away in her sari end. It paid for her fare and one cup of tea. As soon as she reached the town, Roopbala sold her gold chain and bought herself a white sari. She found a secluded place near the river and there she broke the red glass bangles she always wore, cut her long hair off with a rusted razor blade she found on the bank, changed into white and officially declared herself a widow. She was only thirty-one years old. She went and sat down on the steps of a temple by the river and quietly began praying. Now began her endless search for peace of mind. Roopbala went from the small town to Allahabad to Benares to Mathura and finally, to Haridwar. She sold all her jewellery, and when her money finished, she began living on alms.

Wherever she went, however much she prayed, Roopbala saw only her husband breathing his last. He came to her in her dreams regularly, shrouded in his velvet curtain, only his bloodshot eyes gleaming like two pieces of burning coal. 'Tall…witch… demon's daughter…,' he shouted, his voice always muffled and low. Sometimes even when she was awake, Roopbala thought she saw him hovering near her elbow, but when she turned around sharply, there was no one there. Roopbala prayed all day long, asking God for forgiveness. She fasted on religious days and gave away whatever little she saved in charity, but her husband's spirit would not leave her. Roopbala grew thin and emaciated. She began to walk with an awkward stoop, which would have gladdened her late husband's heart had he seen it. A fanatical look had now come into her large eyes and her hands twitched nervously all the time. 'Penance, you have to do penance,' said the head guru of the ashram she had been staying at in Haridwar. 'Go to Badrinathji. There you will find the peace you are searching for. Pray at the Lord's feet and your husband's soul will be set free.'

Roopbala took his advice. She attached herself to a party of three old widows who were going up to Badrinath and they agreed to let her come with them. 'She looks mad but she is tall. She will help us on the mountain roads,' said the leader of the group, a cheerful, plump woman called Bela.

They set off one early morning, the three widows, Roopbala, and one short scowling man who seemed to be an old servant. The women wore white like Roopbala, but they did not seem to be like the ordinary widows Roopbala had met during her wanderings in countless religious towns. These women had an air of gaiety about them which was never seen in widows. They chewed paan constantly, talked and laughed in loud voices, and used strange words when they stumbled over a stone or their servant did something wrong. The leader, Bela, was about fifty-odd years and the other two, whose names Roopbala did not know, because when she asked them they burst out laughing for no apparent reason and said, 'Call us what you want, sister.' There were many other groups setting out for the journey, but Roopbala chose to stay with these women because they asked her no questions and accepted her quickly as one of them. 'Maybe they too have committed some crime and are going to seek forgiveness from Lord Vishnu,' thought Roopbala and a ghastly picture of three slain husbands instantly rose in her mind. She began walking faster. The path was narrow and full of stones but it was so well trodden that the surface was smooth and the stones had no rough edges.

The pilgrims followed the river and Roopbala could often hear loud cries of 'Jai Badrivishal…jai' rise above its deafening roar. They walked slowly, but at a steady pace. The path allowed only one single file and behind them came the mules, loaded with all their belongings. Roopbala did not have anything to bring with her, except for a small bundle of two saris, but the other women had brought with them a huge amount of luggage. Besides their own personal belongings consisting of oils, soaps, clothes and paan boxes, and many other items which far exceeded the limits an ordinary widow is allowed, thought Roopbala, the women also had huge bundles of cloth which they were going to give away to poor holy men on the way, and a pile of cooking pots which clanged at every step the mule took. Then there were dry rations of rice and dal, umbrellas, rush mats and pillows. A big, red cloth bag which contained the prayer books and rudraksha beads was kept separately from the worldly goods, and the servant, whose name was Ganesh, was often reprimanded if the two touched.

The path gradually began to get more and more steep and rocks jutted out at every corner like barriers. Roopbala had to brush aside the overhanging branches too, and she stumbled often. 'Be careful, sister, otherwise the river will take you back to where we came from,' laughed Bela and put an arm out to steady her. They walked till there was light and when the sun had disappeared behind the cliffs and they could no longer see the path, they settled down under a huge rock. The servant was instantly sent off to collect firewood and when he came back, grumbling loudly, showing the women the deep scratches on his arms, they just laughed and ordered him to start cooking. He huddled over the steaming pot, muttering angrily like an old witch brewing her evil potions.

Roopbala sat separately, eating some dehydrated rice she had brought with her, but the women forced her to share the food their servant had cooked. 'All your sins will be washed away soon, so why not eat with us?' said one of them mysteriously. 'Who are these women?' wondered Roopbala once more, as she ate the delicious, spicy vegetables after so many years of just boiled rice. Then mats were spread out on the ground and the women, tired out by the long journey, fell asleep at once. But Roopbala stared for a long time at the dark ceiling of the cave. She could hear jackals howling outside, and the river, glinting in the silvery moonlight, seemed to have quietened down now and flowed much more gently. Small black bats flew in and out of the cave and Roopbala watched their triangular shapes merge into the darkness. As usual, her dead husband's shrouded face appeared before her eyes and Roopbala gave a quiet sigh and went to sleep.

They started off very early in the morning when the light was still dim. A faint mist hung in the air and the path seemed to play hide-and-seek with them. It climbed higher and higher like a spiral of smoke and the women walked more slowly now. They would often stop, and then after taking a few deep breaths, start off again. The river had recovered its earlier fury and now raged below them, churning up waves and crashing them against the giant boulders. 'Do not look down,' shouted the coolie leading the mule. Roopbala looked straight ahead and walked, her knees trembling with fear. To add to her fright, the servant began telling them tales of horror he had heard from other pilgrims. 'One woman, a widow like you, fell down from right here. They found her in Haridwar. Had to cremate her there and then. Luckily, all the family were already present. Saved them the extra journey,' he said, looking pleased for the first time since they had left Haridwar. His good humour continued till they had reached the rock where they were to spend the night, and when the jackals began to howl, he started telling them stories about wild animals. 'There are bears here which attack only women for some reason. Sometimes panthers too come here at night, but if there is a man, they go away,' he said, as he served them their food. He was about to begin another tale when Bela sharply told him to keep quiet. The old man, hurt, walked out of the cave to his own sleeping place just outside, but before going, he cast a look of great horror, as if he could see something they could not. The women could not go to sleep, even though they were weary and their legs ached. 'You go to sleep, I will keep watch,' said Roopbala, feeling sorry for them. Her words seemed to soothe them and they fell asleep after saying their prayers loudly.

Soon the cave echoed with their gentle snores and Roopbala sat up and watched the light playing on the cave walls. She thought of her past life and wondered how it would have been, had she been six inches shorter. Maybe she would have had children by now and would have been busy looking after them. Most of their family land had sold to pay off debts, but the small patch left would have been enough for her son. She could even see him running through the fields, his face a copy of her husband's, but a smiling, happy one, something she had never seen in him. Suddenly, a twinkling, bell-like sound came from the youngest woman's feet and Roopbala saw a quick gleam of a silver anklet before it disappeared under the bedclothes. She was stunned. No widow ever wore anklets or any other jewellery. It dawned on Roopbala that these women were not respectable widows but bazaar women. Maybe they were dancing girls, or rather had been once, because they were too old now. She stared at their sleeping faces and slowly, in that dim moonlight, she began to see them differently. Their white saris changed into bright silken ones, and they lay there glittering with earrings, bangles, anklets, necklaces, nose pins and many other showy ornaments Roopbala imagined dancing girls wore to entertain their patrons. So that is what their sin is. But even then, mine is greater than theirs, she thought, unable to stop a feeling of slight pride creeping into her mind. She decided that she would walk much faster than them tomorrow and would not eat any more of their rich food. 'I am sure they eat garlic and onions.'

She shut her eyes and tried to go to sleep, forgetting her promise to guard over them. As always, her husband appeared, covered by the folds of the curtain, but this time he was accompanied by the three women who danced and swirled around the shapeless bundle. Roopbala watched the mirage play on her closed eyes and was about to fall asleep, when she heard a sudden grunt. She knew this was not a part of the dream because her husband had never made any sounds in her visions of him in the past five years. Roopbala opened her eyes and peered outside. The moon was covered by a fine strip of cloud and the river had turned into molten silver. And then a huge figure loomed at the entrance of the cave. It gave a low grunt and sat down. At first Roopbala thought it was a pilgrim who had lost his way and was looking for shelter. How tall he is, was her first thought. Maybe he too has no home like me. 'Have you lost your way, brother? There is a cave nearby where you can stay. We are only women here,' she said in a kind voice. The figure did not seem to understand what she was saying and was busy rummaging through the luggage, picking up boxes and sniffing them. It gave a low growl and Roopbala suddenly saw two hairy arms rise up in the air. It was a bear, she realized, and her heart stopped beating. The animal was now licking an empty pot and its claws made a horrible scratching sound on the metal. Roopbala watched it silently, not daring to breathe. The servant had said that the animal was scared of only men and she was afraid that it would see her and attack. Then she remembered that she was as tall as a man; her husband had always said so. 'A man she is, not my wife.' Roopbala gathered all her courage and stood up. She grabbed an umbrella and brought it down with all her might on the bear's head. She missed him by a long margin but hit the paan box hard. The clang was so deafening, it seemed to Roopbala that her ears would burst. It echoed again and again, filling the small cave entirely, and a rubble of stones began to slide down from the roof. The women woke up screaming, but the bear had vanished long ago. Roopbala, feeling victorious and happy for the first time in her life, ran out to see where her enemy had fallen. But there was no trace of the animal. A sudden movement in the bushes caught her eye and Roopbala went towards it, not afraid anymore but eager to do battle. 'Oh God, save me…I will never cheat again… save me…I will give up tobacco…gambling…save me…oh God…have mercy…,' moaned a voice and Roopbala moved the branches aside. Ganesh was huddled up, shivering. He had covered his head with leaves and Roopbala reached out to move them aside. 'Ohhh…nooo. I am a woman…only a woman,' he groaned, hiding his head deeper in the foliage. 'It is me…Roopbala. The bear has gone.' Ganesh sat quietly for a few moments and then leapt out of the bush and fell at her feet. 'You are a goddess. You have saved my life.' Roopbala was pleased by his gratitude but did not want to show it.

She brushed him aside and walked back to the cave. 'What was it?' asked the women, their eyes huge with terror. 'Oh nothing, a bear. I chased it away.' As the women gasped in horror, mixed with admiration, Roopbala turned her smiling face to the wall and went to sleep. Her husband's image seemed to have been impacted by her bravery as well, faded away and did not show up again.

As soon as they woke up the next morning, Roopbala asked the women who they were. At first they seemed reluctant to say anything, but after Roopbala said she would be walking separately from now on, they told her their story. 'We were the Raja of Janigarh's dancing girls. All three of us were bought by the Raja in Benares many years ago when we were mere girls. Now we are old and cannot dance or sing any more, but the Raja, a kind man, did not want to throw us out. He gave us a cottage near the palace to live in and told us we could sing devotional songs at his temple. Last year, the Raja passed away, so we discarded our fine clothes and jewels, shaved our heads and came to pray for his soul,' said Bela.

'Do not leave us, sister, you have saved our lives. We were never bad women, just singers and dancers like our mothers were before us, and now we sing only to praise Lord Krishna,' said the youngest one, whose anklet had given the secret away. Roopbala, who was not keen to walk alone, said a few more reluctant words just for appearance's sake and then all of them set off together once more.

~

The path now curved dangerously as it wound its way up the mountain. On one side, the Alaknanda river roared angrily, lashing at the boulders that stood in her way and, on the other side, the steep rocks rose like a wall. Sometimes the path was so narrow that Roopbala could only put one foot forward at a time. They walked very slowly now and no one talked at all, because they were breathless with the effort of climbing. Ganesh trudged heavily behind her, huffing at every step. Whenever she turned around, his eyes looked pleadingly at her, imploring her to keep his secret. Roopbala liked the sense of power conquering the bear had given her, and gradually began to walk tall as she used to, many years ago. The other pilgrims they passed on the way looked at her in awe as if she was some strange, mountain being, and even Bela treated her with more respect now.

The path continued as before, narrow, steep, and strewn with stones, which made it more difficult to climb. Sometimes small stones rolled down from the cliffs above their heads and if they did not jump back quickly, they would land painfully on their heads. 'It is the road they are building for motor cars. That is what makes the mountain angry,' muttered Ganesh as they walked. 'If you want to reach the Lord's feet, you must walk there. What is the use of sitting comfortably in a motor car or a bus and reaching there?

Badri Maharaj is benevolent to all, but I can tell you he will first answer the wishes of those who have walked all the way and then listen to those pilgrims who have come the easy way,' he announced to everyone they passed. The path became more difficult when it rained, but most of the time, the sky was a clear blue and small clouds floated above their heads. It seemed to Roopbala that the same clouds from Haridwar were accompanying her to Badrinath.

As they climbed higher, the air became colder and Roopbala wrapped both her saris around her tightly. Bela and her sisters now began to distribute clothes to the many holy men who sat meditating on rocks along the way. They received their gifts silently and only nodded their heads. But one man, meditating on a lonely rock, his long matted hair falling around him like a robe, shouted at them as soon as they came near. 'Go, you women of the devil, go, do not come here,' he screamed, raising his fist, his eyes shut tightly. The women scampered away but they left two dhotis by his side. Roopbala saw him pick up the clothes and examine them carefully.

'How did he recognize us with his eyes closed?' wondered the youngest sister, her voice full of admiration.

'Must be your stupid anklet, what else,' said her sister sharply.

'Why, it could be the smell of zarda in your paan,' she retorted sharply.

'Old habits die hard,' muttered Ganesh from behind and then looked away sheepishly when Roopbala turned to look at him.

The sisters were more careful now and gave the dhotis only after examining the men. 'He should be very poor and thin. I do not like the look of these well-fed ones. A holy man can never be fat,' said Bela firmly and passed by several men who looked covetously at the bundle of new clothes. The women fed beggars too, and if they found a stray pilgrim, suitably emaciated, they gave him money.

'God has given us so much, we must share it,' said Bela to Roopbala, but when her sister asked for a paan, she snatched her paan box away saying, 'Why did you not bring your own?'

The women quarrelled, sang devotional songs and gossiped with the other pilgrims they met. Sometimes they cried out loudly, beating their chests. 'What a man the Raja was! Give him peace. Oh Lord Badrivishal,' and then Roopbala too began to cry. She remembered her husband's angry face just before the curtain fell on him and her wails grew louder. The women, impressed, glanced at her.

The path now began to grow steep again and they all fell silent. For fifteen days they had walked. Their faces were burnt black by the sun and their short hair now stood as matted as the holy men's. Roopbala's toenail had turned blue and now began to fall off. She had deep cuts on her feet where the sharp rocks had pierced her skin and her face was lined with fatigue. But they still walked on, boasting how much each one was suffering. When Roopbala's nail finally fell off, a sign of envy appeared and each woman looked at her feet hopefully. 'The gods are watching to see how much we suffer, then they will reward us,' said Bela, smiling smugly when her hand was grazed by a thorn. Wild plants grew densely along the path, and when Roopbala looked up, she could see the high peaks towering above. Suddenly, for the first time in her entire life, Roopbala felt small. The tall deodar trees, the cascading waterfalls which fell from great rocky heights, the giant boulders that stood like small hills by the side of the river, and then above them all, the mighty snowcapped mountains, everything had been made for giants, much taller than her. 'This is where I should have been born. No one would feel offended by my height here,' she thought.

After walking for a few more hours, climbing wearily with tired, aching feet, they reached their destination at last. They could now hear the faint sound of bells ringing in the temple beyond and tried to walk as quickly as the narrow, uneven path allowed them. Though it had seemed so near, it was evening when they finally reached the gates of Badrinath. Roopbala could see the lamps glowing in the fading light and from the temple came the sound of a conch shell, as if it was calling her to prayer. She ran ahead, and then, as she bowed her head to touch the cool, stone step, she gave a soft sigh and fainted.

Roopbala lay unconscious and sick for many days after that, but managed to survive somehow. The old dancing girls nursed her through her nightmare and even now that she was well recovered, they sat looking at her with a maternal concern as if she was their newborn baby. 'Eat a little more. How pale you look,' they coaxed, taking turns to feed her, quarrelling over the best food for her. Even Ganesh hovered around, asking her gently if she wanted something, but disappeared as soon as Bela ordered him to do some chore. Roopbala found that they were living in a hermitage not very far from the temple and she heard the soothing sounds of the chiming gongs. When she was feeling stronger, they went for a sight of the deity, and Roopbala sat on the steps and prayed for a long time. The crowds jostled her, and some people, thinking she was a beggar, even dropped a few coins in front of her, but she sat with her eyes closed, deep in meditation. The priests repeatedly asked her for money, but she ignored them and they finally went away muttering, 'Widows are getting too clever these days.' She started coming to the temple every morning at dawn and sat on the steps, praying till the evening worship began. This was the time she liked best, when the smell of incense filled the air, the lamps were lit and conch shells began trumpeting. The low chanting of verses, though she could not understand a word, gave her a feeling of immense peace.

As days went by, Roopbala slowly forgot her past life, and the dark, frightening memory of her husband's dying scene gradually began to fade from her mind. Now when she shut her eyes, she only saw his scowling, stout figure just once in a while. 'Give, Ma, give one anna and you will find a place waiting for you in heaven. One anna, for you, two annas for your late husband, three annas for your parents and four annas for anybody else,' whispered a voice in honeyed tones, as if sharing a secret only with her. Roopbala opened her eyes and saw a young priest sitting nearby and watching her. She had never seen him before; he was too thin to be an experienced priest, but there was a wise look in his small, close-set eyes. She had been in Badrinath for a month now and had only prayed by herself. Now she was tempted to give this young priest one anna in case her own prayers were not enough when it came to getting a place in heaven. Then she thought, why not include the entire family when she was going to pay. They could all achieve salvation together. Roopbala was about to speak to him, then she remembered that she had no money at all. Not even one anna for her own soul. She shook her head sadly and turned away. The priest seemed to understand and did not ask her again.

Roopbala now decided that she would try and earn enough money to buy her family their rightful places in heaven. 'I am here, so it is my duty,' she said. Bela and her sisters had left already, but even if they had been here, she would not have asked them for money. Who knows what would happen if she used that kind of money for the prayers. Maybe God would send her entire family to hell to sing and dance forever, thought Roopbala, a frown of worry appearing on her brow. 'No, I shall wash dishes at the hermitage or sweep the grounds; they will pay me. That is all I want,' she said to herself. She began working from the very next day, and after a few months, earned her six annas for salvation. But the young priest whose face she had found wise was not to be seen and Roopbala did not trust the older, fatter ones. So she continued to work, putting off the salvation ceremony for later.

One year passed, and Roopbala was still washing dishes and sweeping the hermitage courtyard. She had forgotten why she had started working. It seemed as if she was born to do these menial jobs. She had got used to it. She also began cleaning the temple steps on her own and polished them so hard that they shone like silver now. 'What a tall woman. She must be from a warrior caste,' thought the priest and allowed her to clean the outer rooms too. It was difficult to find someone to do this work, and moreover, she was not asking for more than one anna. Gradually, she started selling flowers and leaves for the prayers, charging the wealthy pilgrims, but giving them away free to the poor ones.

One day when Roopbala was collecting the old flower petals to put them under the tree, she saw a stocky man climbing up the temple steps. She stopped working and stood still, her heart was beating very fast. How could this be? Had she gone mad or was God punishing her again for her sins? The man came closer and then sat down on the first step with a loud grunt. His face was turned away from her but she knew without doubt that it was her late husband. Who else could express so much resentment in a single, low grunt? Roopbala's legs began to tremble, but she forced herself to go forward. 'Do you want some flowers?' she asked, her voice coming in a harsh whisper. He looked up at her, but his eyes seemed to be glazed over with a film of cataract. He did not recognize her. Then she noticed he had only one arm. A series of horrifying thoughts raced through her mind as Roopbala stood staring at him. Suddenly a woman came up to them. 'So you are here. How many times have I told you to stay behind me, not walk so fast? Are you deaf as well as blind?' she said in a shrill, scolding voice. Roopbala was amazed to see Gajanath just bow his head and say nothing. 'What has happened to his mighty rage?' she thought. Then they both got up and walked away, Gajanath taking care to stay two steps behind the woman. Roopbala heard her say, 'You were giving the tall beggar woman money, weren't you? You fool. Wasting our money.'

Roopbala wanted to call out to him but she stopped. What was the use now, she thought, and stood silently watching them. The woman was so short that Gajanath, even with his hunched up, cringing posture, looked like a giant next to her. 'God grants all our wishes eventually, but still you can't have everything,' thought Roopbala and laughed. Suddenly she knew she had been set free and let the peace of Badrinath engulf her once more.

6

Rites of Passage

'Mangalik'. Ever since I was a child this word had hung over me like a mysterious and distant threat. But I was not really afraid of it because I was not sure of what it meant. All I knew was that it was a terrible word and it belonged only to me. My mother would say it softly and sigh when she combed my long hair and plaited it each morning. I heard my grandmother hiss it out with anger every time I touched her special silver tumbler and even the servants often whispered it when I was in the kitchen and clicked their tongues in sympathy. Only my older brother thought it was a stupid word and got very angry when anyone called me 'Mangalik'. I knew he was jealous as usual—of me. As I grew older, I began to enjoy the special status the strange word gave me. I even liked its strange sound. The long soothing 'Mangal', a word my grandmother chanted the whole day and then the sharp, abrupt 'ik'.

What was it about this word, I wondered, but never asked anyone in case it was too frightening for me to bear. I wanted it to be a comfortable, familiar fear like the wicked old witch in the stories my grandmother told me or like thunder on a dark, rainy night. Then, when I turned fourteen the word was finally explained to me and it turned out to be a disappointment. All it meant, the priest explained, not to me but to my mother, was that the planets had not been moving in their proper order when I was born and that my husband would die before me. I saw nothing terrible in this, but my mother and my grandmother set up a wailing at once and even the maids joined in. Though the women had always known this is what 'mangalik' meant, it was only when the priest pulled out his tattered red almanac and read out the exact time and date of my impending misfortune, that everything suddenly became official and my mother had to do something to mark the event. So she began beating her chest gently and crying.

After that was over, my father took charge. He called the priest into his study and shut the door on our curious faces like he always did when he entered that secret, forbidden room. As usual, the women rushed to the window and sat down on the mat which was always kept there for them so that they could eavesdrop in comfort. The men began talking. The priest, an awkward young man, overcome by the honour of being allowed into the Raibahadur's special room, started stuttering and mumbling softly. We strained our ears to catch his words and my grandmother, who was slightly deaf, muttered angrily under her breath but did not dare curse him like she did when we mumbled. My father spoke loudly and clearly for our benefit because he hated repeating anything and he also wanted to finish the priest and my mother in one breath. 'I am not a superstitious man as you know,' he said, looking at his bookshelf lined with heavy English journals and the priest too followed his gaze, muttering his ready agreement. 'I do not believe in all this nonsense but what has to be done has to be done. I have read the scriptures from beginning to end and all the ancient sages say the same thing. The "mangal grah" must be averted or else doom is certain.'

The priest coughed once or twice to say that he too shared the same thoughts. My father continued, 'It is written that a girl who is a "mangalik" is cursed to become a widow even after marrying a "mangalik" boy, but another book says that there is a way to escape this.'

Now the priest suddenly spoke up loudly, 'I know…I know… marry her to a peepal tree.'

My father did not like the way this important information was stolen from him and sat in stony silence for a while. The priest realized he had overstepped his brief and hung his head apologetically, in silence.

After a suitable pause to show his annoyance, my father began once more. 'The girl is to be married to a peepal tree and then widowed. In this way the planets are fooled and the curse is averted.'

The priest wanted to add many details to this curt information but he restrained himself. I could see him nodding his head and gulping down his rush of words.

'See to the arrangements and fix a date,' said my father and went back to studying the new English journal which had just come for him from England that morning. The priest stumbled out of the room and was immediately engulfed by the women in a warm, eager, questioning circle. 'What shall we do? You must tell us, Panditji. But first you must eat something,' said my mother and guided him to our sitting room. The priest, regaining his dignity and importance quickly under my mother's kindly gaze, started talking clearly and confidently once again. In fact, he was sounding a lot like my father.

'You will make arrangements for the wedding as soon as possible. All the rituals should be carried out properly, especially the widowhood, otherwise the gods will not believe it has happened,' he said, taking a small sip of the almond-flavoured milk my mother had placed before him. 'I will fix a date for the wedding after consulting the almanac. We will go to the riverside for the ceremony since the wedding and the widowing ceremonies can be performed there easily.'

'Whatever you say, Panditji. Just rid my daughter of this "grah",' said my mother with a deep, sorrowful sigh which, after years of practice, she had become very good at.

'Yes…yes. Do not worry,' the priest replied, also looking solemn. But a tiny moustache of white foam covered his upper lip, giving him the face of a sad clown, and I could not help laughing. My mother slapped me gently to show outsiders how strict she was with me and folded her hands in apology to the priest. After reluctantly accepting a small box of sweets and casting a quick look at the closed door of my father's study, the priest left. My mother and I broke into loud laughter as soon as he was out of the door but were quickly silenced by a gentle cough from the study.

From the next day my mother began preparing for my mock wedding. She ordered the munshi to buy bales of red silk, sequins and English satins and our old tailor was told to move into the small room along the verandah. I was measured a hundred times a day as my mother made the old man open the stitches and remake every garment. 'Make it at least four inches bigger and then fold it. She can wear the same clothes for her real wedding. Why waste cloth?' she said, suddenly turning thrifty. But I was to have four new sets of gold ornaments though my mother had already made plenty of jewellery for me. She would often make me try on the glittering jewels and we both had a lot of fun doing this.

'This is a good time to get money out of your father. He will give readily now so why miss the chance?' she said, her eyes full of love and greed for me.

A dozen red and green glass bangles were bought too and my mother, for the first time, especially asked for the cheap thin ones. 'They have to be broken. The expensive ones will take a long time and your father is sure to get angry.' She also bought one cheap white sari for me to wear when I was widowed but for some reason she kept it bundled up in one corner and would not let me look at it. She kept ordering little things like silver boxes for sindoor, mehndi, red ribbons and gold buttons every day and the poor munshi rushed in and out of the house with her lists.

Everyone in the house was infected by my mother's enthusiasm and her frantic preparations and even my father stopped by on his way out one day to see what the tailor was doing and made him spoil an entire row of stitches! Only my brother kept muttering that all this was a load of rubbish and we were behaving like illiterate people, but since he never had the courage to protest in front of my father, the only literate person beside him, we did not care what he thought of us or my impending wedding. My grandmother too was angry about my mock wedding to the peepal tree, but for a different reason. She did not like the way my mother was enjoying herself preparing for the event.

'First she gives birth to three dead sons and only one live one. Then she produces one girl and that too a "mangalik". Now she is fleecing my son to have jewels made for herself,' she said to the maids every morning when they cleaned her prayer room. She shut her eyes and clutched her prayer beads in her fist angrily whenever she saw me now.

'You think the gods can be fooled so easily? They can see what is going on. They can look down and see that a four-inch hem has been left on the girl's kurta. You think they won't know that she is neither a real bride nor a widow?' she said to my mother every day.

But, as usual, my mother ignored her. She made a pile of new clothes not only for me but for herself as well. She bought a silk kurta for my father and one for my brother, but he threw it back at her and said, 'I don't want to participate in this mumbo jumbo. How can my father, an educated man, allow you to do this to the poor girl? All of you think it is a game, a doll's wedding.' My mother just laughed and pulled his hair and he walked off angrily. The next day he went back to his college even though he still had a few days of holiday left. I was happy he had gone. He was no fun these days, though I liked the word 'mumbo jumbo' that he kept saying all the time.

Three days before my wedding, a halvai was called to set up a temporary kitchen in the courtyard and great cauldrons full of delicious smelling food bubbled and steamed all day. Though no relatives were invited for the event (we were under strict instructions from my father not to tell anyone about my wedding to the peepal tree), my mother's family, who lived in the same town as us, began to have all their meals at our home. My grandmother would watch from her window as they arrived promptly at mealtimes and abuse them softly. They could not hear her and would turn their happy faces to her window and fold their hands respectfully. How much I used to laugh then!

My father, after giving his consent, maintained an aloof silence as usual, but my mother took care to keep the activities away from his part of the house and made sure her relatives did not stray anywhere near his study. Then, finally, the day of my wedding arrived. I was made to bathe early in the morning but only after my mother had rubbed a paste of turmeric and sandalwood powder on my body. 'There is no need to do all this but why not have a proper rehearsal for your wedding?' she said, laughing, and hugged me. She now no longer sighed when she combed my hair though she still called me 'mangalik' in a funny, teasing way.

On the day of my wedding, the entire household got into three tongas very early in the morning and after some confusion and delay because the priest had sat down next to the cook by mistake and in the process, also squashed the huge ball of dough meant for the puris, we finally left the house. All along the way, the priest kept checking his new dhoti, which bore a damp moon-shaped stain on it now. 'Do you think I should bathe before the ceremony?' he asked my grandmother.

'You can bathe a hundred times in the Ganga but you cannot fool the gods,' she said, pointing to the sky. The priest thought she was talking about the puri dough and got even more nervous. He sat with his head bent for the rest of the journey. Was this a bad omen too—like so many others that took place that morning? Afterwards, my mother tried to recall those signs many times. 'What happened had nothing to do with anything that was done or not done by you,' my brother would say, but she never believed him and neither did I. The priest, the planets, the gods, the peepal tree—everyone and everything seemed to have plotted against me that day.

But when we reached the river that morning, the sun shone like a gold and silver disc and everything, the river, the trees and the flowers looked so fresh, happy and beautiful. They were to betray me later, but today they beamed and smiled kindly. The sky was a strange pink, tinged with grey and gold, a colour I had never seen before, but then I had never got up this early in the morning and I kept yawning all the time. My new red silk dupatta did not look as pretty in the morning light as it had done at home and I wanted to take it off. But my grandmother tied it tightly around my waist and told me sharply to sit down in one place. 'At your age I was married for two years already and was not a wild lamb like your mother has made you,' she said, but then suddenly patted my cheeks. 'Remember to give that new white sari to me. Don't put any marks on it. I will give you halva at home,' she said, smiling sweetly, just the way she did when I tickled her feet or when my father scolded my mother.

My mother was busy arranging all the puja things we had brought for the priest and my father sat far away under a large umbrella held by a servant boy. It looked as if he had not come with us at all and was a stranger, but for once he was not reading his English books. Though it was still early morning, it was beginning to get hot now and he asked the priest to hurry up with the ceremony. But there seemed to be some argument about which peepal tree to choose. My mother wanted the tall sturdy one with a dense crown of leaves, but the priest had already selected a slender young one with branches.

'What does it matter? Just get on with the ceremony,' said my father irritably.

My mother had to obey him but she grumbled softly to me all the time as she poured ghee into the havan. 'Now I am sure my son-in-law will be a sickly, thin boy. Why could we not choose the stronger tree? See how shiny and dense its leaves are! Just like your father's hair when I married him.'

The priest ignored her and carried on chanting but my father cleared his throat in a reprimanding tone and silenced her.

The sun had now reached high up in the sky and all the lovely colours of the morning had vanished. The priest droned on till he was ordered by my father to shorten the ceremony and he quickly finished it off with one hastily mumbled prayer. Then he began preparing for the widowhood rituals. The peepal tree's pale grey trunk was smeared with turmeric and ghee and then, after a dramatic pause, the tree—my bridegroom—was cremated with a burning twig. The smoke began to hurt my eyes as the priest started his mournful chanting once more and I burst into tears. My mother laughed and said, 'Oh, the poor thing is feeling sad about losing her husband!' And even my father twisted his face into a thin smile. But the priest did not like my wailing and hurried on with his prayers.

'It is not a good omen,' said my grandmother as she walked up to us. She had been sitting far away under the shade of the peepal tree my mother had wanted me to marry because, being a real widow, she could not attend my wedding. Now that I had been widowed, she could come and sit with us. She pushed my mother away and took charge. 'Fetch a big stone. First break her bangles and then wipe the sindoor off. Cut her hair a few inches,' she barked at the maids.

But my mother would not let her touch me. 'Let us go and eat first. Otherwise all the delicious food we've brought with us for the wedding feast will be spoilt.' She ordered the servants to bring the food out and told the cook to heat the oil for the puris.

'It is too late now, you should have eaten before I started the last rites,' said the priest who had by now turned into an enemy.

'Never mind, we can treat it like a shradh and still eat,' answered my mother, who always won every argument she started except the ones with my father.

The food was quickly brought out by the servants who were as eager to eat as us and before my grandmother and the priest could appeal to my father, the cook, who had kept everything ready, began frying the puris. The aroma of pure ghee floated out onto the clean river air and the priest succumbed to it with a feeble, 'The Brahmin has to be fed in any case.'

After we had eaten and the servants had cleared the dishes, the widowing rituals began. Just to annoy my grandmother, my mother told me to first take my bridal clothes off. The maids held up two sheets and made a tent. My mother slipped the red kurta, now crumpled and sweaty, over my head carefully and folded it. 'You have dropped kheer on it, you silly girl,' she said, but she was not angry. Her beautiful face shone with excitement and I could see that she was quite happy. She took all my jewellery off and made me wear the white sari. It was cooler than the silky bridal clothes but it felt strange. I had never worn a sari before and had trouble walking out of the tent. But when I came stumbling out, no one spoke or laughed and suddenly the happy day became different.

The servants watched with suspicion and fear in their eyes as my grandmother broke my bangles on a stone, and my mother was quiet for the first time that morning. We now sat by the river in a huddle under the larger peepal tree and no one seemed to know what to do next. Long shadows stretched on the river and flies buzzed around my face. The priest too was not sure how long this mourning period should last and watched the cloudless sky as if to ask its advice.

'They are watching,' whispered my grandmother and I thought she was talking about the urchins who had gathered to eat the scraps. 'From heaven, they are watching. It is not so easy to fool them,' she repeated a little louder, and my mother, surprisingly, did not say anything this time. The sun was now high above our heads and a hot, dusty breeze blew around us. My red bridal dupatta unfolded itself from the neat pile and fluttered in the wind. My head ached and I wanted to go home. I whined softly to my mother and she patted my head. 'It is over now. We will go home and you will have lots of sweets and dozens of new red and green bangles.'

But that did not happen. The gods were not fooled. I was married the following year. My husband who, strangely enough, looked a lot like the thin grey peepal tree, died within three months of my wedding. I never wore red bangles again but no one in my family called me a 'mangalik' anymore. They did not call me anything at all.

7

Hiding Away

The grass had changed from green to grey as dusk crept in quietly behind my back. I was hiding once again, this time behind the old gate, waiting for someone to come and find me or at least start looking for me. I hid from my family regularly in places that were secret but not so secret that no one could find me. I had my favourite hiding places, which were scattered not very far from the house, safe places from where I could see the verandah and bits of the garden. I was about eight when I first began hiding and gradually, as I realized the heady feeling of creating alarm in others, forcing them to worry about me, I began to run away even more frequently. At first my mother, our old ayah and my sisters showed a satisfying, genuine fear when they found I was missing. They rushed around the house, shouting, 'Khuku, baby…where are you?' Their voices laced with worry would reach me where I was hiding and my skin would prickle with joy. I loved the way they called out my various pet names; the high notes and the agitated voices gliding towards me filled me with happiness and reassurance. Then, one day, they lost interest. My cousin, who had just returned from the US, told my mother that

I had an attention problem and that they should ignore me. 'She is nine years old, not a toddler with whom you have to play hide-and-seek all day,' said this cousin, who wore gold-rimmed glasses that glinted even in the dark, 'You spoil her, Kakima,' he said, not looking at me.

'I do not spoil her. It's her father,' said my mother, and then they began talking about an English film, using words I could not understand. We were sitting in the verandah watching the fireflies, which had come out for the first time after the rains. The garden, with its stunted flowering trees, looked bigger at night, making my secret hiding places darker and more difficult to find. I was not spoilt by anyone. They just felt sorry for me because I was not as cute and fair and plump as my brother. Sarlama, our old ayah, made special sweets out of gur and coconut for my brother which none of us, except for my father, was allowed to taste. 'Open your mouth, my little Nandgopal, my piece of the moon,' she would say, and pop one glistening brown sweet into his mouth. My brother carried these sticky sweets in his pockets everywhere and then when Sarlama was not looking, he would give me one. But then she found out and gave him some more sweets and made him swallow each one in front of her, coaxing him with soft words.

Everyone loved my brother, not just Sarlama. Even the beggar who came to the gate in the afternoons, crying out in a cheerful voice, 'Give us a coin, one coin for one old man.' He would look straight at my brother, blinking his yellow eyes. Sometimes we lobbed a coin at him, sending it high over the gate since we were not allowed to go out of the house alone. The beggar always jumped up and caught it deftly despite his lame leg. Then he would look at my brother, wink and smile before limping away, leaving a trail of dust. The beggar never asked me for anything and once, when I gave him a banana I had saved for him from lunch, he just slipped it into his large cloth bag and turned away.

The grass beneath my feet now looked like a black rug, with tufts of white gleaming where the street light fell. Maybe I should have hidden earlier, before the tailor had come. I could hear my mother's voice scolding him for making the sleeves of her blouse too tight. I stood on my toes and looked over the gatepost. Sarlama was sitting on the steps of the verandah with a plate. Was she waiting for me? It was getting really dark outside now, much darker than it ever seemed from the house when I looked out of the window at night. The cement gatepost I was leaning against felt cold against my back and when I rubbed my hand on it, the white chalk came off. I could see everything in the verandah clearly, now that they had switched all the lights on for the tailor to check the faults in Ma's misshapen blouse. It was as if I was in a theatre hall, watching a play. One by one they came out into the verandah—my brother, my sisters, my cousin with the glinting glasses—and stood around Ma. They held cups in their hands and my brother looked out into the lawn, pointing at something. Was it a firefly or was he looking for me?

The tailor, having accepted defeat, was preparing to leave. Now my mother would look around and see that I was not there. She would ask Sarlama where I was. Everyone would know that I was not there. Any minute now, they would begin rushing about, calling out for me. I waited, my legs sinking into the grass which seemed to get deeper. A pigeon fluttered on the broken ledge of the gatepost, its wings grey and blurred. Yesterday, the mali had found a snake in the garden. He had killed it with the handle of the lawnmower, shouting at us not to look into the dead snake's eyes. 'It will remember who killed it and come back for them later, when it is born again in another life.'

How long is another life? Why don't they ask for me? 'See Ma, I'm here. I am hiding here,' I tried to shout, but my voice was stuck in my throat. The gatepost pushed against me, cold and white, making me sink into the grass. The darkness gathered around me tightly and I felt I could not breathe. Waves of fear and panic rose in my body, holding me down as I tried to move towards the house. Then everything—the house, the garden, the brightly lit verandah—everything disappeared. My hand, which I held in front of my face, was a line of black. We were all lost, each one of us, as I had seen before in so many nightmares. I would never find them again because they would not know who I was anymore. I could search forever, but never find my family, my house, the arid garden, the verandah with five cane chairs, the steps where Honey's pups were born last week, the sandboxes with the footprints of a thief who stole my mother's gold necklaces. I tried again to call out to Ma, to my brother, to my sisters, but I could not remember who they were. Fear engulfed me and I could not remember my own name.

'Khu, Khu…Khukoo,' sang the sweet voice from behind a beam of light. I ran towards it, suddenly free of the darkness. My father stopped the car at the gate and called out again. 'What are you doing here in the dark, you silly girl?' he said, scolding me in his soft, tired voice as I held his hand. The house was lit with candles and my mother came down the steps, her sari-pallav floating behind her like an angel's wings. 'The lights have gone off again. Why are you roaming about in the dark? Had your milk, Khukoo?' she asked absent-mindedly, patting my head. I still held my father's hand, but not so tightly now. The fear ebbed away, leaving no traces. I had forgotten the darkness, though the garden was a sheet of glistening black shadows now. It was as if I had never been afraid, never felt the cold despair that had wrapped itself around me just a few minutes before. My father let go of my hand, but I could still stand. When he died eleven years later, I reached too late to see him, to hold his hand—to thank him for finding me even though he did not know I was lost. After that day, I never tried hiding again. Instead, I found new ways to seek attention but a fear of darkness, of being alone, still shadows me.

8

In Possession

The market was a long way off. If she sent him now it would give her enough time to cook, throw the food out and wash the dishes. There would still be enough time left for any suspicious odours to float out and leave the kitchen as untouched and clean as before. Having taken the decision, Sheila felt much better. The endless morning, looming heavily ahead, suddenly acquired a sharpness and she knew the day would pass quickly. She swung her feet off the bed in one swift movement and peered under the bed for her slippers. She did not put on the old rubber chappals which made soft, squeaking noises when she walked. Instead she chose the low-heeled sandals which made a satisfying clatter on the cement floor. They always gave her a feeling of authority.

Hiru heard her footsteps, though the kitchen was far away from her bedroom and separated from it by a courtyard. He was cutting onions and thought at first that it was the sound of the knife on the wooden chopping board. As the footsteps became sharper, he stopped and tilted his head to listen. It was her. Hiru wiped his hands and waited. Sheila now came into the passage that led into the kitchen and paused near the doorway. They faced each other. The old cook stood straight, his face half turned away from her, the knife poised in his hands. Sheila did not go into the kitchen. 'Hiru, please go to the market and get some watermelons…today,' she said and though she tried to speak slowly, the words came out in a rush and formed an incoherent, breathless sentence. But Hiru heard her clearly though he did not answer at once. He began chopping the onions again. His hands moved at an incredible speed and as Sheila watched, the knife became a blurred silvery line.

'Today is Friday. I go to the market on Tuesdays,' he said, without looking at her. Sheila was prepared for this. 'Sahib wants to have watermelon for breakfast tomorrow morning.' A clear lie and both of them knew it. She felt her breathing becoming faster as she waited for Hiru to make his move. The smell of onions was making her eyes water and she shifted her weight to lean more towards the kitchen. Hiru raised his head and looked at her. His right eye was covered with a fine, white film of cataract and the clear one looked abnormally large and bright. Sheila suddenly felt nervous. What if he refused to go? Then she would have to tell Dev and she did not want that. It would add a totally different angle to the situation. Sheila was not prepared as yet to take things that far. The tension between the old cook and her was so devoid of any tangible proof that very often she thought that she had imagined it.

~

Hiru was never rude, never disobeyed her orders, but his hatred of her was as solid as an iron wall. What could she complain to Dev about? 'I do not like the way he stands' or 'why does he look at me blindly like that.' Dev would not understand her fears, shadowy even to herself, and it would confuse him and make him unhappy. If Hiru refused to go to the market then she would have to go back to her room and think of some other way of making him go away from the house. But he had already taken down the shopping bag and was waiting for her to give him the money. She came into the kitchen, quickly put a few notes down near the chopping board and hurried back to her room. She would now have the kitchen to herself for at least a couple of hours. Hiru's old bicycle would take him to the market at a, thankfully, slow pace and it would give her enough time to try cooking something new. Everything she made turned out to be inedible but she could not throw it in the dustbin outside the kitchen. Hiru would know what she had done. So Sheila had to walk to the end of the garden to throw the food across the hedge and soon a heap of rotting food piled up there which the flies circled but the stray dogs did not touch.

Sheila waited for Hiru to leave the house and then went back to the empty kitchen. She walked around, opening the drawers one by one in an aimless way, without seeing what was in them. She rearranged the various jars and bottles and then put them back again as they had been. She picked up the knife and began chopping the onions Hiru had left on the table, trying to imitate the quick movements of his hands, but failed and laughed at herself. Whenever she managed to send Hiru away and came into the empty kitchen, it gave her a strange feeling of jubilation. She remembered herself as she had been before she came to live in this house and it made her happy.

It was very rarely that she had the house to herself, though she was alone in it for most of the day. The old cook, though she could not see him, was always there, watching her. Wherever she went in the large house with its maze of musty, dark rooms, she knew he had been in the room just before her and would come in as soon as she left. The silent conflict between the two of them had begun very soon after she had come into the house and after one year, it had now settled into a secret battle which only they knew about. The surreptitious war had rules which both of them obeyed. They had divided the house between them and moved around deliberately like pieces on a chessboard, trying to dislodge each other. Sheila had felt the old man's dislike as keenly as a sharp slap the minute he had looked at her with his white, faded eyes. 'This is Hiru, our old cook. You won't have to worry about anything, he does everything,' Dev had said to her as soon as they had entered the house. The old man, silent-footed, had followed them as they walked through the house to Dev's mother's room. He watched Sheila without looking at her. When they reached the door, the old man suddenly rushed forward and went in, as if to warn Dev's mother about her.

Was it only a year ago or much longer, she could not remember clearly anymore. She opened and closed the kitchen drawers without thinking and began searching for some vegetables to cook. She would try to make the eggplant curry Dev was so fond of. But Dev only liked it the way Hiru cooked it. When she had cooked a dish for him the first time many months ago, he had eaten it politely, praising her cooking after each mouthful till she wanted to cry. 'Why don't you let Hiru do the cooking, why should you bother?' Dev had said later in the evening.

Sheila began to wash the eggplant under the tap. She noticed that Hiru had pasted a small faded picture of Dev as a boy, on the shelf near the sink. Dev's face, round and solemn, faced the camera while his half-turned body looked as if it was about to run away. Hiru had obviously tried recently to take the photograph off because it had scratches along the edges, but the picture had remained stubbornly stuck, fading slowly in the sunlight. Sheila wanted to tear it out and throw it away along with all the other things in the kitchen that belonged to Hiru, but was afraid to do so. That would be breaking the rules. She could only fight him without words or gestures. She could only claim this house as her own by stealth and cunning, like a ferret hunting its victim only by sound. She had her small victories, like today, but they were few. This house belonged to Hiru. Her mother-in-law had never owned it, nor had it ever belonged to Dev. Hiru was its owner, its protecter, fixed on it as firmly as a gargoyle. She knew she could never take the house away from him. Still, she kept trying to steal it from him for a few hours by sending him away on long, useless errands. She would then walk around the empty house, enjoying her freedom from his ever-watchful eye or she would try to teach herself how to cook in the kitchen, which was forbidden territory. Hiru somehow knew what she had been doing in his absence because he always scrubbed the kitchen as if it had been contaminated as soon as he returned home.

Hiru had come to work in the house when he was ten years old. His only job then was to clean the rice every morning and polish the sahib's many pairs of shoes. The memsahib would often ask him for rice grains with husks and both of them would sit in the courtyard all day feeding the sparrows. Sometimes she fed the birds small bits of broken biscuits and would give him one or two to eat also. They had tiny silver balls on them and the birds would never eat them. Gradually, Hiru began to follow the memsahib as she walked around the house. He carried various things for her and gave them to her as she needed them. Soon, like a well-trained nurse in an operation theatre, Hiru learnt to hand over the odd assortment of objects at the right moment, without being asked. He carried her two pairs of spectacles, one for reading and sewing and the other for looking far away to see if the sahib's car was coming, a small sewing basket, an old book heavily bound in red cloth, which was the Gita and must never be put on the ground.

Sometimes he would also carry a sari with a half-stitched fall attached to it, which trailed behind them as they walked around the house, along with half-finished letters and a book with a feather stuck in between the pages. The memsahib talked constantly to him. At first he did not understand what she was saying because she talked of such strange things. She was only a few years older than he was, though he did not know that then, so she spoke to him like an equal and assumed that he would understand what she was saying. Gradually, the words began to fall into a familiar pattern and Hiru could make out many sentences which made sense because the lady repeated everything many times over. Since she never wanted a reply or asked Hiru any questions, he felt free to understand her words in any way he wanted. As she talked about her father, her various childhood friends and long-forgotten journeys, Hiru would give to these unseen people and places his own images. Her father Hiru saw as a tall man with a deep voice, her friend, Beena, who appeared in the stories regularly, he saw as a gentle, pretty girl, while the other friend who was rarely spoken about, Hiru saw as a thin, unfriendly girl. The memsahib, who had soft brown eyes and was not much taller than he was, would smile at Hiru as she talked and sometimes they would laugh loudly together when the sahib was not at home. The other servants went away after they had finished their meals and there was no one else at home during the afternoon except the two of them. Even when the sahib came home, in the evening, they would sit together on the verandah steps and talk softly while the sahib read a pile of papers.

~

Nothing changed even when Dev baba was born and the three of them would share stories which Hiru now knew by heart. He used to go home for a month during the summer, but every year he came back a few days earlier. 'Hiru, this house frightens me in the afternoons. Come back quickly,' she would say each time he was leaving. One summer, Hiru was late coming back because his uncle had chosen a girl for him and he had to get married before he left. He worried about the memsahib and baba but he felt too shy to ask the village letter-writer to write to her about the wedding. When he reached the old house after three days of travelling, he ran straight up to her room. She and Dev baba were sitting quietly on the bed. 'We have been waiting for you every day, Hiru,' she said and the three of them began talking at once. Baba gurgled while the memsahib began telling him about the snake that had been killed in the garden and Hiru told her, in a low voice, about his bride.

As Dev baba grew older and began walking, a young girl was brought from Raniganj to look after him. Hiru was amazed that the sahib could think that someone else could take care of baba while he was there. 'It is only when you go home, Hiru. You know the memsahib does not keep well,' the sahib had explained, but the next year there was no need for him to go to his village ever again. His young wife, whose face he could not remember, had died in a fire that had burnt their village hut to the ground. The kitchen where he had grown up was now his only home, the baba and memsahib his only family. He looked after them as possessively as a she-wolf with cubs, allowing nobody else within this circle of care. He knew better than they did what their needs were. When Dev baba was sent away to a boarding school by the sahib, the memsahib and he were alone again and now she needed him even more. But she did not talk to Hiru now and spent most of her days in her room or walking in the garden. She smiled at him in the old way but instead of telling him stories, she would sing tunelessly to herself. He would see her from the kitchen window wandering in the garden touching the trees, speaking to them. The other servants laughed at her at first, but after Hiru told them that she spoke to God through the trees, they watched her silently from afar.

Dev baba would come back for a few days and then they would sit together in the courtyard. But now only Dev baba spoke and they listened with joy to his loud, newly broken voice even though they could not understand most of what he was saying. Hiru tried to picture the words as he used to do with his memsahib's strange stories but failed. Then Dev baba went away to a foreign country to study and did not come back for many years. The memsahib grew more silent every day and now never came out of her room and even when the old sahib fell ill one night and was being taken to the hospital, she refused to see him. He died a few days later and when they brought him home, Hiru had to explain to her why this flower-bedecked body was lying on the living-room floor. Dev baba came home for a few days and then went back again after the funeral ceremony was over.

The memsahib did not speak to him at all while he was there but after he had gone away, she would call out his name repeatedly when she was alone in her room. Now she often did not recognize Hiru and called him by strange names. Sometimes she would giggle like a girl and try to hide behind the curtain when he went to give her tea. The factory was taken over by a relative of the memsahib's and Dev baba wrote to her every week on postcards which had bright, colourful pictures on them. Hiru put them carefully in a drawer in the kitchen. Long ago he had found a picture of Dev baba as a small boy and pasted it on the shelf above the sink. The face in the picture was how he saw Baba in his mind even though he had changed almost beyond recognition. Time went around slowly like a circle, without a beginning or an end and Hiru grew old along with the memsahib. All the other servants had left and the furniture in the house was covered with white sheets and the doors remained closed for days since nobody ever came or went out from the house.

Then Dev came back one day and with him was this girl. Hiru was reluctant to take her into his memsahib's room but she followed Dev. She smiled at her as if she knew her well and then put her hand out to touch the girl's face. The girl drew back sharply with a nervous laugh. Dev baba came forward and stood between the memsahib and the girl. 'Ma, I have got married. This is Sheila.'

The old memsahib continued to smile but Hiru was stunned. She had talked to him for years about the kind of girl she would find for Dev. 'She will be like a princess, fair with big black eyes, Hiru, but humble and kind. I will give her my diamond bracelets as soon as she gives me a grandson.' Hiru would laugh because Dev baba was only a year old and he could not imagine this fat, gurgling baby ever having a wife. Now she stood before him, a thin girl with a pointed face and dirty feet. The memsahib's feet were like white marble with fine blue veins and Hiru suddenly felt a deep rage in his heart. They had been cheated, both the memsahib and he.

~

Sheila turned the tap off and began to dry the eggplants. She should hurry though there was still an hour left before Hiru got back. She would leave the kitchen before that and be safely in her room. She picked up the knife and slowly, with unsure hands, began cutting the eggplant. How long could this hide-and-seek go on? Sometimes she felt a rising hysteria and wanted to scream at him. But the words only rushed through her head and would not come out. But today, she felt different, much stronger. Suddenly she decided she would not leave the kitchen when Hiru came back. 'Let him see me here. From today I am going to stop this cat and mouse game. He is not going to frighten me anymore,' she said loudly to Dev's faded photograph. 'This is *my* house, *my* kitchen,' she muttered again and again, like a sacred chant as she opened a cupboard and took down a frying pan from a row of gleaming vessels. How clean everything was, almost like a hospital.

Sheila remembered how the old servant had stared at her feet on the day she had arrived. She had told Dev that she wanted to have a bath and change her clothes before meeting his mother, but Dev said it would not make any difference. And then as she stood before the old lady, she realized why. Dev's mother, with a face as beautiful and fragile as a porcelain statue, was a total vegetable. She smiled gently and then reached her hand out. Sheila felt embarrassed that she had flinched when the old lady tried to touch her. But how could she know what she was going to do. Dev had never warned her that she was so far gone. Senile people could be violent sometimes, she had read somewhere. The old servant was staring at her in a strange, fixed way, as if he was trying to memorize her face while the old lady had already turned away to look at the garden. What a pair. Sheila felt a sudden urge to laugh but controlled herself. Dev might misunderstand.

They had been married only a month and had known each other only a short while before that. Dev was polite and considerate to such a degree that it was already getting on her nerves. When she first met him, Sheila had liked him at once. He came to their house with her brother, following him into the room like a large friendly dog. He sat down on the nearest chair available, folding his large figure into a comfortable shape. He had sat there quietly the whole evening while her family swirled around him in their boisterous way as if they had known him for years. Sheila was intrigued by this awkward man, who, though the same age as her brother, possessed an elderly, slightly weary manner. She tried to get him to talk about himself, but it was such a strain for her that she soon gave up and told him all about herself instead. It was wonderful and rare to have such an attentive listener amongst them and everyone wanted to talk to him from all directions. Sheila was certain that they had frightened him away and she would never see him again, but to her amazement he came back the very next day. He chose the same chair, moulded himself into it and within seconds her family was clinging to his chair like drones around a queen bee. From then on he would come over and sit in her house day after day, placid as a pool, surrounded by their chatter.

One day he came early and found Sheila alone. She was surprised when he asked her to go out with him and they began to meet each other alone every day and Sheila got to know more, but still tantalizingly few details about him. He was the only son of a wealthy family, his mother was an invalid and he had lived in hostels during most of his childhood. He had been studying abroad for the last five years and was now on his way back to Raniganj, a small coal mining town, to look after his late father's factory and his invalid mother. That was all that he would tell her.

Sheila was intrigued by his quiet, almost secretive manner, but what she found most attractive about Dev was the way he listened to her. She could not resist the way he sat still for hours, his head tilted at a slight angle, his kind eyes resting on her as she talked. She heard her own voice more clearly when they sat together like this and it pleased her greatly. When he asked her to marry him, she said yes without stopping to think. They wanted a quiet wedding since his mother was too ill to travel and her father, who did not like attending noisy, crowded family functions, agreed happily. 'No vulgar showing off,' he said. 'No expense either,' he added later when Dev had left.

They had come to Raniganj right after the wedding and Hiru had been waiting for them at the gate.

The old house, which had seemed so beautiful and mysterious on that first day, gradually began to close in on her, inch by inch, week by week. She was alone at home all day except for Hiru and the old lady. She only saw Dev late in the evening. He still listened to her as attentively as before but his eyes often looked tired now. Sheila sometimes saw her mother-in-law, whose rooms were on the other side of the house, standing near a window, but when Sheila went to meet her, Hiru came out of nowhere and took her away. He took care of the old lady as if she was a child, just the way he looked after Dev and the house. He was everywhere, all the time. He would wait for Dev at the gate no matter how late he returned home from the factory. Sheila would see him from her window, sitting on his haunches on the low garden wall, his white uniform gleaming in the moonlight. He did not smoke or chat to the chowkidar, just sat still for hours and then sprang up when he heard Dev's car. He cooked for Dev, washed his clothes, while hers went to the dhobi; he even decided what Dev should wear every day and laid out his clothes neatly on the bed every morning. Sheila tried to shake off her anger and irritation by making fun of the old man's obsessive devotion, but Dev was so surprised at her that she never did it again.

She wished her brother was here, then they could laugh about Hiru and he would become just a harmless old man. His eyes would lose their piercing gaze and the house would not seem so oppressively full of his presence. But her family had forgotten her totally. She, who had once been the centre of every activity at home after her mother had died, was now not even worth a letter. She had been married for a year now and her father had written to her only once. It was actually a letter addressed to Dev, asking him for a donation for a local charity and to her, his favourite child, he had sent a lottery ticket with a note scribbled in the narrow margin. 'Keep the money, return me the rupee, love, Pa.' Sheila never replied. Dev was her family now and this old house full of shadows and pigeon droppings, her only home. But it did not belong to her. Sheila gradually grew more and more silent. Her voice, once so clear, so fluent at turning the ordinary into a melodrama now turned flat. After being silent the whole day, she found that when she tried to speak to Dev in the evenings, she tripped over words as if she had just learnt to speak the language. She tried to read but her attention wandered. Hiru seemed to be always watching her from some unseen hidden corner.

But he was not going to anymore. Today she would end this tiring battle which was driving her mad. What if she became like the old lady one day? Today she was going to turn her back on his hatred and make this house her own. Sheila lit the stove and threw the matchstick on the spotless floor. She poured some oil into the frying pan and then opened her recipe book to find out what to do next. The oil was sending out a thin spiral of smoke and Sheila couldn't find the page she was looking for. In a panic, she threw the onions into the frying pan and a loud hiss filled the silent kitchen. The oil spluttered angrily, turning the pieces of onion black. Sheila tried to take the frying pan off, but the heat made her recoil and move back. The smoke had now reached the ceiling and through the haze, Sheila saw Hiru standing at the door.

A sudden rush of fear made Sheila tremble. She had done nothing wrong. This was her house. He was only a servant. He was paid to obey her. Sheila turned the stove off and faced him. 'Hiru, clean this place,' she said, almost shouting. Hiru looked at her blankly, as if he could not recognize her. Then he came in and began washing the charred pan. His hands scrubbed the blackness out slowly. 'Memsahib…,' he said almost in a whisper, 'the old memsahib is dead.' Then he wiped his hands and waited for her orders, a sad, broken man she had feared for so long.

9

Lost Garden

It was almost dusk and the path to the garden was covered with a fine mist. Leela walked slowly. Suddenly her foot hit a stone and she almost stumbled. Why had she not seen the stone before? Maybe she had, and had forgotten about it. Her memory played tricks on her these days. It was like playing hide-and-seek with herself. She remembered some odd things clearly, while important things like newspaper headlines she forgot as soon as she put down the paper. But even when she was younger, much younger, she forgot her mother-in-law's birthday and her neighbours' names with astonishing regularity, and her late husband, D.N., always said she was doing it on purpose.

The early autumn breeze, floating down from the higher hills, touched her face with cool hands. The peach trees shed a few golden leaves as a greeting and sighed. Leela turned back to the house. She must be careful. That is what her children said to her whenever they visited her, ate the delicious food Amlu had cooked and then took what was packed for them in tiffin boxes. 'Ma, you must be careful at your age. Anything can happen,' they warned as they drove away in a cloud of dust.

Leela had fallen off a tree when she was seven years old and broken her hand. At sixteen, she had seen her uncles killed in a riot as they fled their home during Partition. She had had mumps, measles and chicken pox when she was twenty. At thirty, she had undergone a major operation. She had been robbed several times, got stuck in a lift, been in a flood, an earthquake and a fire. Now, at seventy-eight, she wondered with great interest what else could happen to her. The lights were on as she walked into the living room. Her three servants, Amlu, Babbu and Sunil were watching television. They rose as soon as they saw her, but they all kept their eyes fixed on the television screen. A large man with a false moustache was being chased around a bed by a knife-wielding woman. She was dressed in red and heavily bejwelled as if she was going to a wedding. 'Not suitably dressed for murder,' thought Leela and walked out again. She had obviously entered at a crucial stage of their favourite serial.

Leela always wondered what these simple hill people who led quiet lives thought about the violent family feuds they showed on television. But when she asked Amlu, who had been with her for twenty-five years, the servant-woman just shook her head and laughed. 'They do many strange things, these people. There is always something bubbling in the pot in their homes. You want to see what will happen next.' Leela understood this waiting and watching. That is all she did nowadays. Wait and watch. She opened her bedside drawer and took out a book. It was a small, hard-cover diary with a silk cover. She opened it carefully. The pages were brittle and yellow with age and the faded-ink writing almost transparent. Leela gently turned a few pages and began reading loudly to herself: 'Warm, bright day with a south-west breeze. The cool weather is slowly coming to the garden and today

I will plant fifty seedlings. The mali says too early but he always says that to annoy me. I shall plant them myself. R. does not like it when I work in the garden. He says the servants will think we are bringing down their prestige. English memsahibs have to behave in a certain way laid down in 1857 when the Crown took over from the East India Company. Working with your hands in the garden is not something they allowed us. Seventy years later not much has changed. Anyway R. is away on a long inspection of the Shimla hills and I shall do what I please. I think a mixed border of phlox, pansies and baby's breath will look nice near the fountain. The mali will plant them in a straight line, I know. He hates a mixed border.'

Leela closed the book gently and smiled. The malis had not changed in the last hundred years. The diary was dated 1928 and, though most of the writing had faded, she could make out the author's name clearly—Mary. She never wrote her last name though and always called her husband 'R'. Must have been Robert. That was a popular British name during the Raj. So noble.

Leela wanted to plan a garden just like Mary's but she could not find all the flowers she had mentioned. Some were English wildflowers Leela had never seen, but Mary seemed to find them all over the garden. Since there were no records of the house or the land surrounding it, Leela did not know where Mary's garden-boundaries were. She often spoke of a fountain but Leela had never seen any fountain in the garden. Her father had bought the house from the former Raja of Banethi, who had bought it in 1947 from a British couple. Someone had obviously destroyed Mary's fountain.

'Another glorious summer day. Went for a walk along the stream. There was delicious-smelling wild thyme, marsh buttercups, and near the rocks there were clumps of pink clover. Dog roses and honeysuckle are getting ready with hundreds of buds. Soon the air will be fragrant with their heavenly scent. I am waiting for the wild iris to sprout. If we have some good showers, these clever little plants will cover the entire hillside behind the house. Saw a blue and grey butterfly. I must look it up.' She had painted a small butterfly, but the colour had faded to grey now.

For every month Mary had a different poem, but most of them were a bit sad. Many of them spoke about birds and flowers of the English countryside:

A cloudless sky;
a world of heather, Purple of foxglove;
yellow of broom, We two among it, wading together.
Shaking out honey, treading perfume

She must have been very homesick and maybe a bit lonely too. She did not have any children it seemed and her husband was always going away for some lengthy tour of the Shimla hills. Maybe she loved being alone, enjoying the solitude of her garden. She did not seem unhappy, just a bit wistful. Then just as she was writing about going out to gather wild irises blossoming on the hillside, she stopped. The last page in the diary was just a curt line. 'Leaving for home. R. will follow later.' It had no date so Leela would never know when she left India and why she did not plant her irises.

~

Tomorrow she would take Amlu and walk to the end of the garden. If she walked slowly she would not get tired. She remembered seeing a bench there once. She and D.N. had walked there to check the bench, but there was a beehive close by and D.N. did not want to linger. 'Too many blasted wild creatures hanging around in the garden, Leela. Moles, bees, sparrows, hares and foxes. You should tell the servants to get rid of them. Put more stone slabs in to discourage all this nature business getting out of hand,' he said in his loud voice. But he had gone long ago and the creatures still thrived in the garden. 'Is the stone bench still there, Amlu?' she asked when Amlu brought her morning tea. 'I do not know, memsahib. Shall I send the mali to check?'

The bench was still there, but surrounded by a thick clump of grass and a few sparkling daisies. 'Be careful. There are grass snakes here, I am sure,' said the mali, hacking at the grass with his scythe. A delicious scent of fresh green grass filled the air and made her sneeze. 'Oh. You are cold. We must go back,' muttered Amlu, clicking her tongue like a worried hen.

'No. It is all right. The grass made me sneeze. I am fine, Amlu, I will sit here for a few minutes,' Leela said. The mali quickly cleaned the bench for her and she sat down slowly. She was a bit tired and breathing heavily, but she smiled to show them she was feeling fine. 'Walked to the end of the garden. Saw a pair of white birds and a yellow and orange butterfly. Lots of daisies in the grass,' she thought in her mind and laughed. 'I am beginning to think like Mary.' Amlu and the mali smiled too and nodded at each other. 'They probably think I am getting a bit soft in the head. Maybe I am. But it is a nice, peaceful feeling,' she thought, as she watched the light dance on the leaves. A green woodpecker suddenly gave a shrill call from a pine tree above her and then began pecking at the tree trunk again as if in a great hurry.

'When do the irises come out on the hills?' she asked the mali, who after half-heartedly clearing the weeds around the bench, was now sitting on a fallen branch, gazing at the forest. 'Must be waiting for his lunch break,' thought Leela.

'I do not know any iris flower. We have never planted it in our garden,' he said and began chewing on a blade of grass. Amlu had disappeared, but Leela knew if she coughed or sneezed she would be behind her at once like a genie from the lamp. 'Irises are bluish purple and they grow all over the hillside,' Leela explained.

'I never saw them. No English flowers on the hillside. Only jungli plants we must never bring to our garden. They have poison and will kill all our pretty flowers,' said the mali with a firm shake of his head and cast a proud glance at the garden. The lawn, kept weed free and brilliant green by him, shimmered in the sunlight. A row of brightly coloured flowers grew obediently within neatly painted white brick borders. Not one dared to cross the line. The mali would pull them up at once. Leela coughed and Amlu appeared at her side like a spirit. Together they walked back to the house, the mali leading the way like a happy mascot. 'Be careful, memsahib, many stones here,' he said and briskly cleared the path for her.

Leela found a picture of a bunch of iris in bloom and showed it to the mali the next day. 'This flower grows all over the forest. But our goats do not eat them,' he declared in an officious tone as if his goats were the ultimate authority on suitable plants for the garden.

'I want to plant them. Just a few,' said Leela and heard her voice turning girlish and pleading. D.N. would have just thundered an order and the mali would have obeyed at once with a look of admiration on his face. 'Just one or two,' she repeated, showing him the picture of an iris once more to tempt him.

He looked at the picture, but kept quiet so Leela was not sure whether he had agreed or not. If she had been ten, maybe twenty years younger she would have walked to the hillside and ventured deep into the forest to search for the irises. Why had she never seen them when she could have gathered them?

They came to Shaya every summer, but the children were small and they liked playing in the garden. Anyway D.N. did not like her going into the forest. 'Too many wild things there. Either take a gun or stay in the garden.' Leela gazed at the hills from her chair. There must be hundreds of irises growing there wild. If she could just plant one in her garden. Just one iris for Mary and her to share. It had been too late for Mary and who knew, maybe it was for her too. In her diary, Mary did not say much about the winter months except who came to visit and a brief description of the changing colours of the leaves: 'Large flocks of rose-finches on the apple trees. The leaves have curled and turned yellow-red. Soon they will cover the ground below. The whistling thrush does not sing very loudly now but I hear an occasional gurgle now and then, as if it was trying to remind me it was still amongst us,' wrote Mary. Leela had begun to hear the whistling thrush. It must have been singing in the garden all these years, but she had never heard it. She saw the tiny watercolour Mary had made of the bird in her diary and now she recognized it whenever it came to the garden. She must plant an iris for Mary. It was Mary who talked to her, who made her see the colours, hear the songs, and catch the scent of new leaves in the drifting breeze. Yes, she owed her an iris.

It took a long time for the iris to spread in the garden, but soon it was happily tripping all over the flower beds. The mali had reluctantly brought a handful of bulbs from the hillside and planted it in the far corner of the garden as if he was ashamed of these wildflowers. But after one good shower, the irises skipped and danced all over the garden. Now the mali seemed proud of them and often showed them to Amlu. It had been a long winter and Leela was too frail to walk to the lawn now. She sat in her chair in the verandah all day and one by one the irises came out in a blaze of purple to greet her and Mary.

10

To Shimla in a Tonga

One bright, warm morning, sometime in 1908, Anima decided to wash her hair on a Wednesday instead of the usual Monday. This ordinary everyday decision changed the course of her destiny and made her travel from the quiet, peaceful town of Benares to the glamorous capital of the Raj, Shimla. On the fateful morning, Anima came out on the roof and began drying her long mass of hair in the sun. She stood there, tall and elegant, shaking her heavy tresses from side to side to dry them faster and began humming softly to herself. From across the terrace, hiding behind a lace curtain, a bright-eyed, handsome face watched her silently. Then, slowly like the sun's rays passing through a heavy cloud, the intense admiring glance leapt over the clothesline, pierced the discarded frame of the string bed, raced across the rooftop, and forced her to turn her head. Their eyes met and it was the first love-match of the new century. Ananda knew at once that this was the girl he was going to marry and take with him to Shimla. Once he had made up his mind, everything fell into place as if by heavenly accord. All the hurdles that should have been blocking such an impulsive, unorthodox match where the boy and the girl had already made up their minds to marry, even before the elders had met and discussed their horoscopes, made dowry arrangements, and hundreds of other details, vanished magically. The girl's father, stunned by the audacity of this forceful young man who had come from some place out of the blue to ask for his daughter's hand, had no choice but to agree. He kept up a forbidding exterior, but secretly he liked the young man, and moreover he had five more daughters to marry. Anima's mother did not give in so easily and kept warning her husband that no good would come of this hurried match.

'Who is this boy? Who was his grandfather? Where is his horoscope? Why does he not want any dowry?' she asked again and again from behind the bamboo curtain when Ananda came to their house. But the wedding took place on the earliest available auspicious day that month and before the mother could gather support amongst the relatives against the boy, they were safely married by sacred, if somewhat rushed, rites. She was helpless to do anything now except cast dark and foreboding looks at the young couple who wallowed shamelessly in their new-found happiness. 'I never thought my own daughter could shame me like this,' the mother lamented to sympathetic relatives who gathered like vultures as soon as they had heard the scandalous news.

It was a relief to everyone when Ananda announced that his job in Shimla had been confirmed and they had to leave immediately. 'It is a bad omen, I am telling you,' sighed his mother-in-law and the relatives. Though they did not see how a well-paid job in the secretariat could be an evil sign, they agreed with her, shaking their heads in slow, gloomy half-circles as they drank their tea. The young couple left Benares quietly one evening by train and except for Anima's cousin brother and Ananda's friend, from whose rooftop he had first seen his bride to be, now declared an enemy by her family, no one came to see them off at the station. Anima's mother had wept copiously when she left home and clutched her to her bosom. 'There are tigers in Shimla. This man is taking you to the wilderness to kill you,' she cried. Suddenly she thrust a small velvet bag into Anima's hands. 'Take these gold beads. But do not tell him.'

The first thing Anima did when the train left Benares was to show her husband the gold beads. 'Keep them safely, but you will never need them. I will earn enough to keep buying you as much gold as you want,' he said proudly, though at the moment he had only ten or fifteen rupees in his pocket. The other passengers in the crowded third-class compartment heard him and shook their heads in admiration. They liked the dignified handsome young man and his tall, slim wife, whose face was as beautiful as a marble statue of a goddess. They kept offering food to the young couple, along with generous advice for a life of wedded bliss. 'Be sure to cook the food he likes,' whispered one middle-aged lady in Anima's ears as she turned around to reprimand her husband. 'I told you not to bring this big trunk. But did you listen? No. Who am I, after all?' she hissed angrily and then started talking to Anima again in a kind voice. 'Husbands are like babies, so helpless. Look at mine,' she said and once again sharply rebuked her husband for bringing the wrong trunk. The mild-looking gentleman just smiled quietly each time she scolded him and then fell asleep with his mouth open.

The train rattled on and the vast plains of north India swept past in the darkness. One by one all the passengers fell asleep, slumped against each other like one large affectionate family. Suddenly a harsh, grating voice spoke out in the silence. 'No. No. It will not do. Beware.' Ananda sat up quickly. He thought for a moment that one of Anima's relatives had followed them surreptitiously into the train, but then he heard a deep snore and saw that a man, curled up in the upper berth, was talking in his sleep. 'No, no,' he mumbled again, carrying on his nightmare battle and turned over restlessly. Relieved, Ananda dozed off again, but Anima, slightly perturbed by this ominous warning, could not sleep. She watched her husband's handsome profile and his perfect nose and fine eyebrows and gradually began to feel reassured. She leaned back against the hard wooden seat and waited impatiently for Kalka to arrive. The train raced through the night, leaving a trail of black smoke which disappeared into the dark sky. Sometimes a burning cinder would fly out from the engine ahead and set the grass along the tracks on fire, but then the rushing train would blow it out in a second. Anima could taste the coal dust in her mouth and her eyes hurt when she blinked.

The night seemed never to end, and Anima wondered if the train had forgotten to stop at Kalka and was now hurling them to some unknown destination over the mountains. Finally, she too was overcome by the drowsy, lethargic atmosphere of the compartment and fell into deep sleep like everyone else. But she woke up much before anyone else and sat quietly, not daring to move, in case she disturbed the lady who was dozing peacefully but heavily on her shoulders. As she watched, the sky turned lighter and slowly, dawn broke far away on the horizon, turning the coal dust on the bars of the window into a silvery powder. In that faded, hazy light, Anima suddenly saw a shaky line of mountains far away. Then after a few minutes they were in Kalka.

All the tiredness of the journey left her and Anima rushed out of the train even before Ananda could help her out. Then she stopped suddenly in her tracks and looked about her in wonder. The small station was teeming with smartly uniformed British soldiers who strutted up and down the platform calling out cheerful greetings to each other. Nearby stood frowning and important-looking officials who, in turn, were surrounded by a small army of servants, coolies and worried babus. From the first-class compartments, pale and delicate European ladies stepped out nervously, their long dresses trailing in the coal dust, and Anima suddenly felt as if she had come to a strange, new country. She had seen Europeans in Benares too, but they were just a few ragged-looking travellers, not splendid, proud creatures like these. Though they passed quite close by her, she seemed to be invisible to them and one lady with pretty blonde curls even leaned her umbrella against her briefly as she stopped to tie a ribbon on her hat and then ran ahead with quick steps, calling out gaily to another friend. Ananda got their few belongings out and then they quickly moved on, following the crowd, and found their way out from the third-class exit gate.

They stood uncertainly on the sloping road and watched the other passengers walk away briskly. Anima knew something was bothering her husband because he had suddenly lost his self-assured manner and was chewing his new trim moustache, which he had begun to grow as soon as he had got the job, in a worried, distracted way. 'There is the new train, we can go in it…but,' he left the sentence hanging in the air. Anima knew at once what the problem was. He did not have enough money for the train tickets. Should she offer to sell the gold beads or would it hurt his pride? mused Anima, afraid of taking the wrong step so early in her married life. 'We can go by tonga, but it will take much longer,' Ananda said, not looking at Anima.

'What is our hurry? The tonga will be better. The train is new, it might roll off the mountains,' said Anima, speaking very fast. They both knew that the brand-new railway line built at an enormous cost was the pride of the British government. There was no danger of it falling off the mountains, at least for the next hundred years, but they kept silent and walked towards the tonga stand outside the station.

It was drizzling gently but persistently when the tonga set off and the narrow, curving road glistened like a snake with a brand-new skin. A long line of tongas travelled together and a few bullock carts trailed at the end of the convoy. Most of the women passengers were sitting in the covered bullock cart, but Anima had insisted on travelling in the tonga with her husband. Ananda was once again impressed by her show of independence and looked at his eighteen-year-old bride with a new respect. Though she was ten years younger than him, there was an air of maturity about her which never failed to surprise him. She had defied her parents and married him. Now she was following him to an unknown place without any murmur of protest and was calmly undertaking a difficult and maybe even dangerous journey as if she had done it all her life. Ananda felt slightly awed by her quiet strength and silent fighting spirit. He himself had been a rebel from a very young age and defied his orthodox father by learning English. Such a scandalous and shocking thing was unheard of in his family—the priests of the oldest temple in his home town for generations and also learned Sanskrit pandits.

Scholars came from all over India to have complicated texts explained and his great-grandfather had written a lengthy, highly acclaimed discourse on the grammatical forms of Sanskrit. But Ananda learnt English, and as if that was not bad enough, he even began teaching himself Urdu from books, since no maulvi could come near his house. His father, red-faced with embarrassment and humiliation, prohibited his son from reading anything but Sanskrit, and one afternoon when he caught him on the roof with Milton's *Paradise Lost,* he gave him a sound thrashing with a cane. The entire village came to see the public flogging and were impressed with the way the old man swung the cane on the boy's back. 'This will get rid of the English madness,' said Ananda's father, happy to have a chance to display his anger to the village.

That night Ananda ran away from home, taking only his English and Urdu books with him. He roamed around various cities, doing any clerical work he could find. He taught the children of wealthy families, translated manuscripts, and even worked as a prompter in a theatre company. But all the time he was studying and improving his command over English and Urdu, and finally one day, his efforts were rewarded. A senior British officer heard of his talents and gave him a job as a translator in the secretariat. From then on he rose rapidly, and today he was going up to Shimla to join the Commander-in-Chief's office as a translator. He had been on his way up, but had stopped in Benares to visit an old friend and then destiny had stepped in and Anima appeared on the rooftop. She sat there now behind him, eagerly watching the breathtaking, strange, new scenery that had dramatically appeared as soon as they had taken a few winding turns after Kalka.

Anima had never seen mountains before and could not imagine that trees could grow to such a height. She took a deep breath, inhaling the spicy, fresh scent that filled the air. The tonga clattered on ahead and the bells around the horse's neck jingled softly, clashing with the sharp sounds of its cantering hooves. As they climbed up, the tonga blowing its shrill, unmusical horn at every corner, the forests became more and more dense and she could only see broken patches of sunlight filtering through weakly.

It was much cooler now and Anima pulled the end of the thin cotton sari she was wearing closer around her. The road seemed endless and the mountains moved further away as they climbed. The sun suddenly dropped behind a tall peak and the road now turned silver-grey in the fading light. 'We shall stop here for the night,' announced the tonga-driver, an angry-looking man with a curling beard, which flew about wildly in the breeze when the tonga moved fast. He pointed to an old, red-roofed house and then disappeared into the darkness.

Ananda took charge and helped all the passengers from the other tongas and bullock carts, up the steep, slippery path. The house had only one large hall, divided by a bamboo screen where all of them crowded in, men on one side, women and children on the other. They spread their rolls of bedding on the floor and lay down to rest their aching backs. A long wooden box stood stolidly near the doorway and the passengers eyed it suspiciously. What was in it? Was it an empty coffin or contained some late Englishman's body? Each one of them wondered anxiously, but none spoke out aloud in case it tempted the evil spirit out of the box. They spent a restless and uncomfortable night, listening to the wind howl outside and watching the box nervously. Once or twice they heard faint scratching sounds and they hoped feverishly that it was a panther lurking outside and not the Englishman trying to escape from his final resting place. Only Ananda seemed to be oblivious of any ghostly presence, and in fact, sat down on the box to put his shoes on, much to the horror of the other passengers. They left the room as soon as it was light and went and sat by the roadside, gloomily watching the beautiful, dew-drenched dawn.

At last the tonga appeared and they clambered in, and soon, to their relief, they had left the coffin far behind. The horse, now fresh and rested, raced ahead at a brisk pace, its clattering hooves breaking the silence of the mountains. Silver-haired monkeys stared at them from treetops and Anima suddenly saw a bright blue bird flash by. They passed a village where they made a short stop; all the children rushed out to see their tonga and an old woman brought hot tea in earthenware cups for them. For two paisa, she gave them crisp puris and a generous amount of potato curry. Then they were back on the road, shaking and swaying as the tonga lurched around dangerous curves. Sometimes wild cats, their yellow eyes gleaming, appeared across the road and then languidly stepped back into the shadows of the forest. 'Evil spirits, these cats,' called out one lady from the bullock cart lumbering far behind and folded her hands in prayer. A jackal suddenly appeared in front of the tonga, but then disappeared quickly, its handsome, silvery-grey head bowed in embarrassment for mistaking them for some edible creature. For two days they travelled like this, spending the nights at small wayside village huts where they made sure no coffins waited to share the room with them. Though the women were full of chatter when they had left Kalka and exchanged minute details of their lives at home, now they sat silently, their voices weakened by the journey and also by the innumerable quarrels that had taken place during the journey.

Tired and weary, every bone in their body aching, they reached Shimla when the sun was about to descend into the mountains. As soon as Anima caught a glimpse of the gleaming red-roofed houses set crookedly on the hillsides, the huge deodar trees with branches that drooped sadly, she felt she had come home at last. The small town looked strangely familiar, though she had never been here before and Anima knew just exactly where the road was leading to as they walked towards the Kali Bari, the local rest house for all Bengalis visiting Shimla or in transit. Ananda left Anima there, and though tired after the long journey, he rushed to the office. His old efficiency was restored once more by the heavy advance on his pay, which the clerk at the office had reluctantly doled out after saying, 'Don't make a habit of it. Sahib does not like borrowers. Never even gives his pen to anyone.'

Ananda quickly found a house and moved his wife out before the priests at the temple could ask her too many questions about his family. Though she would not be able to answer them, Ananda was afraid that the beady-eyed old men would somehow manage to ferret out whose son he was and then he would not be left alone ever. Once, earlier, he had been caught by an old woman who had known his lineage by just looking at his face. 'You are my sister-in-law's sister's family priest's son,' she had exclaimed and fallen at his feet. Ananda did not want that to ever happen again. He made sure from then on to stay away from his community and was pleased when after they had settled down in their small house, Anima, though she was polite to the other women who lived nearby, kept her distance. Her neighbours, eager to welcome this beautiful young bride, and give her their protection and advice, found her aloof and uncommunicative. The matrons of Shimla shook their heads disapprovingly and whispered amongst themselves that she was too beautiful to make a good wife or mother. 'These kinds are always trouble. Remember Ganesh's wife? She too was a beauty, as fair as a memsahib. Within six years of the wedding she had run off with her daughter's music teacher,' said the chief lady of Fagli and the others agreed, nodding with evident glee and malice. But as time went by and Anima showed no inclination of running away with anyone, they gradually became fond of this silent, graceful girl. They stopped and talked to her whenever they saw her on the road and some women even came to ask her advice on household matters, even though she was much younger than them.

~

Years passed by. The First World War rumbled and then became silent far away and Shimla soon grew into a crowded, bustling town as more and more families moved up from Delhi and Calcutta. Each week the train would bring in new batches of pale Europeans and dusky Indians, and while the former strode in, happy to be in a place 'as cool as home' after so long, the latter stood in long queues, answering several queries before they were allowed into Shimla. 'Name? Father's name? Where have you come from? Where will you go back to?' was barked out in quick gunshot sentences. Most travellers answered quickly without hesitation and passed the test, but some who were too startled or frightened to answer back as smartly and swiftly were made to stand aside and vetted later by higher authorities. Once they were let in, the Indian families stayed in Shimla from April to September and then moved down again with the government to spend the winter months in Delhi. Anima did not much care for their small, dark house in Delhi and waited impatiently for winter to pass so that she could come back to Shimla once more. Life was never disrupted by the yearly move, since their entire world moved with them. Schools, shops, offices, servants and even friends shunted up and down the mountain road together. Anima bought groceries in Delhi but haggled and paid for them in Shimla, since the same shopkeeper came up with them. Enmities and friendships too continued without any break and each time the change gave them all a fresh lease of energy. Anima and her three daughters now travelled by the toy train and the journey was no longer a never-ending weary adventure.

Ananda was happy except for one fact. Anima refused to learn English. He tried his best to persuade her to speak in this rich, wonderful tongue, for which he had abandoned his family and home, but she set her lovely lips in a stubborn line and turned away quietly. 'Why should I learn English? Who will I speak it to?' she thought. She did not want to have anything to do with the British, who lived a totally separate life far above them in the higher peaks of Shimla. Anima had often heard strange tales about them; how they had parties where men and women danced together and music came from a special, not the marching, kind of band. They went for something called 'picnic' at Annandale and played games like children, hitting with small hammers at a wooden ball or play-acting. They rode horses, even the women, at top speed around the hillsides and pedestrians had to quickly move out of their way. Anima had once been frightened by one such rider, lost her balance, and slipped down the deep gutter. The lady had stopped to help her up, but Anima had quickly hidden herself behind a large deodar tree till the lady had gone away, muttering, 'How odd...I was quite certain...did see her...' The women in Fagli got their information about the English memsahibs not from their unsporting taciturn husbands who worked for the English sahibs, but from an old shawl-wallah who went to sell his wares to the memsahibs. He would describe, with great drama and enjoyment, each and every detail about the English ladies and their homes to his rapt audience and paint such a fantastic, unreal picture that Anima thought the man was lying. But then once when she stepped aside to allow a line of rickshaws taking English ladies to a party pass by, and saw the pink-and-white doll-like figures, dressed in clouds of lace and silk, and smelt the heady perfume that filled the path, she began to believe the shawl-wallah's tales.

Anima not only found the English people strange and alien, she was also a little frightened by them. Once Ananda's colleague, a large, friendly young man, had decided to walk home with him and had even come into the house, much to Ananda's joy. But Anima had hidden behind the kitchen door till he had left. Ananda was very disappointed and hurt but he did not say anything to his wife.

It was soon after this that the English ghost made his appearance and began to follow Anima around. The first time she sensed his presence was when she was walking back one evening from the Mall. It began drizzling and Anima decided to take a shortcut through the deodar trees and turned away from the main Cart Road which she usually took. The path was moist with raindrops and the dark branches drooped heavily as if sweeping the earth. It was so silent that Anima could hear the water dripping from the leaves and her footsteps sounded unnaturally loud to her. Anima was not a nervous person, but something in the air made her uneasy and she began to walk faster. Then, behind her, slowly and imperceptibly, came the sound of footsteps. She did not turn around but her heart began to beat loudly. She was almost running now. The footsteps seemed to come closer and suddenly a soft voice whispered, 'Edna'. Anima looked back quickly, but all she saw were the sadly drooping branches of the deodar. The path, winding around the hillside gently, was silent and empty. Must have been the breeze, she thought, and looked straight ahead. 'Edna, dearest…please come back to me,' said the voice sharply, sounding a bit peevish now.

Anima picked up the hem of her sari and ran as fast as she could, and did not stop till she had reached the main path. Suddenly she heard voices again, but to her relief they were speaking Pahari.

She knew all the ghosts in Shimla were English, but she felt better when she saw four stocky Pahari coolies coming down the hillside. She asked them whether they had heard the strange voice too, but they shook their heads and said, 'No, but we were busy talking ourselves. Ghosts only talk to people who are alone,' and one of them added, 'Anyway, there are so many ghosts in Shimla now, standing at every corner, whispering away. How many can you listen to? These poor souls must be remembering their own land, that is why they cannot remain happily buried in our soil,' he explained, shaking his head sadly, as they walked away.

Anima did not tell anyone about this incident, quite sure she had mistaken the voice. But it suddenly spoke to her after a gap of a few days, when she was alone at home, and then after that continued to haunt her so relentlessly every day that she got quite used to it. 'Edna…Edna, please…' it would whisper whenever she was alone. It followed her around the house as she did the chores, stood next to her while she cut vegetables, peered over her shoulder as she cooked, sighed heavily when she went to wash clothes. Anima wished it would say something more than just 'Edna, Edna' but it did not oblige her.

In a strange way, the voice made her lose her fear of the English and she began to learn how to read and write the mother tongue of the ghost. In fact, one day, she even said, 'What do you want?' sharply to the voice as soon as it began its monotone of 'Edna, Edna'. It never spoke to her again.

~

Years rolled by and it was 1930 now. The country was going through great upheavals as it struggled for independence, but Shimla remained aloof and above it all. Anima's three daughters had grown up now and sang 'God Save the King' at school every day and spoke fluent English with their father. Ironically, all three of them looked exactly like Anima's mother, who still continued, in her single-minded way, to warn her against Ananda. The girls, plain and sullen, had the same dismal expression of impending doom on their faces and often spoke in sharp tones to Anima, as her mother used to. Whenever they walked together, Anima, slender and elegant as ever, followed by her three squat, frowning daughters, the matrons of Fagli would never fail to remark with loud, unkind laughter, 'What ugly daughters you have produced, Anima? What use is all your beauty?' The girls did not take kindly to this public humiliation and refused to walk anywhere with their mother, saying, 'Why can't you be fat like everyone else's mother?'

Ananda too was now spending less time with her as he climbed the ladder of promotions with dizzying speed and soon became a senior officer. Anima, left alone, slowly found herself getting more and more involved with the freedom movement. She had been secretly giving money to a friend who gave shelter to freedom fighters hiding from the British authorities. She had also learnt to spin with the wheel, but only worked at night, when her family had gone to sleep. Now she read the newspapers every day and as there were many words she did not understand, she asked her daughters to explain, but they impatiently shrugged her off. Ananda, who was so keen once that she should learn English, was not enthusiastic at all anymore and looked angrily at her when she asked him what Civil Disobedience meant. Anima continued to read on painstakingly and even began talking to the women of Fagli about the freedom movement taking place in the rest of the country, but most of them did not seem very interested. 'I want the country to be free, but I do not want to throw my French saris away and wear khadi,' said one matron to Anima and that ended further patriotic talk. But there was a handful of women who listened, and one old lady, with crooked, arthritic fingers, even learnt to spin from her.

One day Anima heard that Mahatma Gandhi, who had been in jail for a long time, was coming to Shimla to address a public meeting. Ananda knew about it too and told her that being an officer's wife she could not attend it; but she had already made up her mind to disobey him. Taking a garland of cotton-thread reels which she had spun herself, she quietly left the house as soon as evening fell, and walked up the Ridge where the incitation was going to be held. She was very excited but sad too that no one from her family was with her. She had not wanted to defy her husband and was sure that in his heart he too wanted to go. Suddenly, she saw the old lady she had taught to spin step out from her house and walk hurriedly towards her. 'Anima, hide your face. Otherwise our husbands will lose their jobs,' she whispered, pulling her sari over her head. Shrouded like ghosts, they reached the place of the meeting. A circle of policemen on restive horses had created a barrier all around but they quietly slipped through and sat down. Bapu spoke in a tired, gentle voice and she could not understand most of what he said. But everyone listened with rapt attention and she saw that many had tears running down their cheeks. When he finished speaking, Anima wanted to go up to him to give him the garland, but before she could move, the police charged through the crowd. Anima got hold of the old lady who had lost her spectacles and dragged her away to safety. They trudged home wearily, their saris torn and streaked with mud, but full of happiness for having heard Mahatma Gandhi speak.

Ananda was awake, pacing up and down the outside the gate. He turned his face away when she entered the house. They did not speak to each other for many days, but then after one week, Ananda declared a truce by bringing a rose-pink chiffon-georgette sari for her. He waved it nervously in front of her as if it was a white flag of surrender. Anima's heart melted and she took the peace offering from him with a shy smile. It was many years since he had bought her anything. But then Ananda suddenly dropped the bombshell that she had to go with him to the C-in-C's party in honour of some visiting dignitary from England. Anima knew she was trapped and could not get out of it without a major battle. Her daughters shouted with excitement and even the servant looked impressed. They ran out to spread the news and the matrons of Fagli responded with envious cries at once. This was the first time that anyone they knew had been invited by the chotta latt sahib.

Ananda did not see any need to explain that it was a last-minute invitation, issued because the guest list had run short of the required number of brown faces. 'There will be senior English officers and their wives, many Maharajas, princes and generals. Maybe the Viceroy himself will come,' he said, excited as a child, but Anima sat silently. What would Bapu say if he found out, she thought worriedly. But she knew she had to go to the party, now that the entire family was egging her on. Like a goat being led to slaughter, she bowed her head and meekly obeyed her husband. For the first and last time she vowed, as she tied the slippery georgette sari and covered her neck with jewels. When she stepped into the rickshaw, Ananda gasped in surprise. She looked just like an English memsahib, but a hundred times more beautiful with her black hair and flashing eyes. Even the rickshaw-wallah stared at her dumbly, though he had seen her so many times before.

When they reached the gates of the C-in-C's residence, Ananda jumped out of the rickshaw and smartly offered her his arm just the way he had seen his boss do. But Anima stared at him in surprise. 'What happened?' she whispered anxiously. 'Has a spider got into your shirt?' Ananda put his arm down sheepishly and they both walked, with hesitant steps, into the lawns of the imposing, intimidating house. As far as her eyes could see, Anima saw nothing but shimmering white figures in strange clothes, who looked as if they had stepped out of a mythological play. The men wore many medals and the women glittered with jewellery. One lady even wore a tiara. Anima had seen such people when she passed the photographer's window on the Mall, but these were even more stiff and remote-looking. A small crowd of Indian ladies stood in one corner nervously as if they were about to be shot by a firing squad. None of them spoke a word of English and they were petrified that some English lady, or worse still, man, would come forward and attack them in the foreign tongue. They silently repeated the few words that their husbands had forced them to memorize and waited for the dreaded axe to fall.

But happily for them, no one approached them, and when Anima stepped into the group, she was greeted with hysterically cheerful voices. 'Come…come, Anima, stand with us. You look like a real memsahib today,' said a thin, heavily made-up lady, giving her a quick, envious glance. She was surprised and not at all happy to see Anima at such an important gathering where only the seniormost officers had been invited, and her lovely looks made matters worse. Anima stood awkwardly, staring down at her hands. A bearer with a large silver tray strolled by them and the lady lunged forward and picked up a glass. 'Arrey, Lata, are you going to drink the water here?' asked the other ladies, aghast at her rash behaviour. But Lata ignored them and recklessly took a large gulp from the glass after uttering her husband's oft-repeated words, 'We should change with the times,' and then adding, 'Nothing wrong,' to give herself courage. But something definitely was not right because as soon as she finished the sentence, she suddenly gave a stifled scream and clutched her throat. Her eyes rolled upwards and she made strange, gagging noises as if she was strangling herself. 'Oh, ooooh…God. I'm dying,' she gasped.

The ladies realized that she needed help but they were not sure what kind. 'It is the wrath of the gods,' whispered a lady, another senior officer's wife standing next to Anima. Lata was now panting with her mouth wide open, as if her insides were on fire, and she twisted her head from side to side. Anima fanned her with her sari-pallav, wiping her forehead, which was now a glistening mess of sweat and face powder. Anima gently guided her to a row of chairs nearby and both of them sat down.

'It was not water…it was…Oh God…what have I done,' cried Lata in a hoarse voice, breathing heavily. A strange, unpleasant smell, almost like medicine, came from her as she spoke, and Anima, repulsed, moved back quickly. 'I will get you some water,' she said, getting up. 'No, no, not water again,' screamed Lata in a hysterical voice, speaking, for some strange reason, in English. Then suddenly, 'I absolutely agree with you,' a man's voice said just behind them and a tall, heavy Englishman appeared out of the bushes. 'Never touch the stuff. Bad for one's insides, my father used to say,' he whispered, as if sharing a secret with them. His pink face was shining with good humour and friendliness as he looked at them. Anima did not know what to do and she stood still, nervously twisting her sari. Lata was sitting with her head bowed, still groaning, and the other ladies had drifted away as soon as the

Englishman had appeared. Anima desperately tried to think of some English word to say to this man but all she could remember was Civil Disobedience, and before she could say anything, the man spoke again. 'I say, where is that chap with the drinks? He had this turban. Can you see him?' he asked now, peering into the crowd in a furtive way, like a man lost in a vast desert with no water in sight. His face suddenly broke into a wide smile of relief as he spotted a glimmering turban in the midst of a group of people standing not too far away from them. 'Ha, reinforcements at last. Excuse me, ladies, be back soon,' he said and moved towards the turban with long, eager strides, his hand already stretched out in happy anticipation.

Anima watched him anxiously. Somehow she felt he was heading for disaster and she wanted very much to help him. There was a loud thump as he brought his hand down heavily on the turbaned man's back. 'A whisky…not too much water…bad for you…my father…,' he said but stopped abruptly when he saw that the man carried no silver tray, just a gold-topped cane in his hands. 'Harold!…His Highness, the Raja of Sabanpur…Your Highness…this is…Lord Charwin, just arrived here…,' stuttered an elderly, red-faced English gentleman in an agitated voice. Anima turned away horrified, as the man, whom she now regarded as her only friend at the gathering, shouted, 'That is jolly good for you, old man, but where is the whisky?'

People had now stopped talking and the English ladies were whispering to each other, their eyes gleaming with suppressed excitement. Anima saw Ananda at last and began walking hesitantly towards him. But before she could reach him, a heavy footstep fell behind her and a voice said, 'Edna dear, wait for me.' Anima's heart stopped. She had not heard the voice for so many years and she now quickly turned around to greet it as if it were a long-lost friend. Her shy smile froze as she saw a huge, fat man with many medals on his chest waddle up towards her. His head was as round and bare as a newborn baby's and a pair of large, bulging blue eyes darted about, looking out nervously for someone. 'Edna, wait,' he cried again as Anima's heart filled with disappointment. This could not be her ghost. How could this man with a toad-like face be him? Her ghost was a tall, thin, sensitive soul with a face like Lord Byron, whose picture Anima had once seen in her daughter's English book.

She forgot about searching for Ananda and stared at the impostor, feeling resentful and cheated. But then out of the twinkling darkness came a tall, thin English lady, and caught hold of the man's arm. 'I wish you would not stride off just like that leaving me alone with that drunk,' she grumbled in a low tone. 'But, Edna, I was looking for you. These medals are suffocating me,' the man said and both of them disappeared into the crowd, muttering softly and irritably to each other. Anima, relieved to have her equilibrium restored, walked behind them, hoping she would find Ananda. She was feeling quite annoyed with him and decided to repeat the English lady's sharp words she had heard just now, when she saw him and quickly began translating them in her mind.

But Ananda looked so happy when she found him surrounded by a group of important-looking men, including the imposter and his wife, that she kept her anger for later. 'Let us go home now,' she whispered. But he did not hear her words and continued to listen with rapt attention as the Englishmen talked. She caught the word 'Gandhi' and at once began to listen carefully too. Her English was not good enough to understand what they were saying, but she still managed to make some sense of the words. Her heart began to beat faster and a feeling of intense rage ran through her. 'Not fit to rule…madman,' she heard, and before she knew what she was doing, she gave the man a sudden push with all her strength and ran out blindly towards the gates. She could hear a babble of voices behind her but she kept running. An arm suddenly barred her way and Anima shut her eyes tightly, waiting for a gunshot. But there was only a rustle of silk and a faint scent drifted up her nose. She opened her eyes and saw an elderly English lady with large brown eyes looking at her anxiously. 'Are you all right, dear? I apologize for Harold. His hands get a little frisky when he sees a beautiful woman. I am glad you gave him a good jolt of iced water. He won't forget it in a hurry,' she said, smiling kindly at Anima. Tears welled up in her eyes and she wanted to explain to this lady why she had pushed the man, but her English failed her entirely and all she could remember was the line her daughter had taught her at home, 'Thank you for your kind invitation.'

She did not speak at all during the rickshaw ride home but Ananda watched her face, made even more beautiful by the moonlight, glow with silent rage. When Anima reached home, the first thing she did was to take off her pink chiffon-georgette sari, tear it calmly and methodically into small strips and then set fire to it in the kitchen. Feeling much calmer after that, she then bathed quickly, and dressed in a cotton sari, sat down for the first time to spin in full view of her family. Her daughters watched her nervously, their eager questions about the party frozen on their lips. Ananda did not come into the room where she sat, but he felt her anger following him through the house, scorching him as if she had turned into a heap of burning cinders.

Anima only wore handspun clothes from that day on and never went to any party again. Ananda did not ask her to accompany him even when the Viceroy invited them. Then one day, many years later, Anima asked herself whether she could accompany him to a celebration. It was 15 August 1947.

11

Friends Forever

The day everything changed forever, Kamala woke up late. The woodpecker was calling from the peepal tree. Her father had already lit the fire and she could smell hot rotis on the tava.

Kamala had come to Setpur from the village to live with her father after her mother died four years ago. She was twelve years old now and quite tall for her age. All the girls in her village were tall because from the day they were born, they drank water from the mountain spring. Her father, who worked as a guard at the English sahib's house, said the spring water was blessed by the forest gods and they should be thankful forever to the mountains, trees and rocks.

Kamala missed her village and her friends. She used to play by the stream all day, pick wild raspberries and chase butterflies in the meadows. When she felt hungry, she could run to the nearest home and eat with the family.

Here they lived all alone in a big house which her father called 'the bungalow'. 'We are lucky to live here. See how big the garden is. Water flows from the taps and we have a strong roof over our heads,' he would say.

Kamala preferred her small hut with a slate roof and wooden floors, but she kept quiet. There were only five other people in this huge compound. The English sahib, to whom she had to bow and fold her hands each time he passed by, the cook and the mali. There was a small English boy and his amma too, but she hardly saw them. The lady was not his real mother but someone who looked after him.

Then there was Amir, the cook's son, who appeared from time to time with fruits, vegetables, chickens and rabbits for the sahib. Sometimes she saw him in the garden. Amir played with a ball while the English boy sat in the verandah and watched.

'Why does the sahib's boy always stay indoors?' she asked the amma one day when she came to their side of the house to hang out clothes to dry.

'Because he is a poor, motherless child.... The stupid dhobi has run away. What will we do? They are all running away. We should have left long ago, I keep telling the sahib. All English people have gone. God only knows what will happen to us. Muslims running there, Hindus running here,' the amma muttered to herself and went in.

Kamala wanted to say she was motherless too but she played outdoors, went to the market, and helped her father to do the household chores, but the amma had already left.

Kamala wished she could go into the big house one day. Baba said there were many pretty things in the rooms, but she must never go in. Sahib would not like it.

~

The storm rose out of nowhere. One minute she was sweeping the little patch outside their room and the next minute a mountain of dust blinded her. She could hear men screaming and shouting and she heard gunshots outside the gate. It was very frightening. 'Baba, Baba,' she called, but she could not see him anywhere. The gates were wide open. Then through the dust she saw a tonga cart drive into the garden, the wheels rolling over the flower beds. Five or six men jumped out and ran into the house. One of them stopped for a moment and fired a gun in the air. 'Come out you coward, let us see your face,' he yelled. Kamala heard a scuffle inside the house and someone screamed. Then one by one they began dragging everything out. Carpets, clothes, furniture….

Kamala hid behind a tree and watched. The English sahib would get very angry but he was not here. Only the little boy was standing all alone in the verandah and crying. His amma was nowhere to be seen.

One of the men brought out a big marble statue and began loading it in the cart. The others laughed at him. 'Leave that, you fool. The police will catch us if we roam around with that thing. Next you will want to take that crybaby too.' 'Come on, come on,' one of them shouted. 'That stupid sahib will be back with the police. Hurry, this was a waste of time. This angrez hardly had any silver. That wretched cook has fled too. Hurry, hurry, we can still catch him.'

Kamala watched them ride out through the gates, firing their guns. Where was Baba? He had a gun too. He should have protected the house. Had the men hurt him? She ran around the garden shouting, 'Baba, Baba,' but only the crows answered her. Then she heard someone moaning. The sound was coming from inside the house. The moaning got louder and louder. 'I must go and see. Someone needs help,' she thought and ran up the verandah steps. There was broken glass and water everywhere. The front doors were wide open. At first she could not see anything because it was dark inside. Then slowly her eyes made out shapes. The chairs and tables were upturned. Broken vases lay in pieces on the floor.

When she saw the body her heart skipped a beat. Kamala forced herself to go closer. The amma lay on the floor, a deep gash on her forehead. But she was not moaning. It was the little English boy who was hiding under the table, hugging a blanket. He stared at her like a scared rabbit and despite everything Kamala wanted to suddenly giggle.

She bent over the amma and tried to wake her up. 'Amma, are you all right? Open your eyes.' The woman sighed and lifted her hand. 'Water,' she whispered.

'Thank God you are alive. Wait, I will get you some water.'

She looked around, but she could not see any water jug. There was no surahi or matka in the room. Then the boy whispered something. Kamala saw him pointing to a big white iron 'box'. She ran there and opened the lid. Inside there were bottles of water as cold as ice. She sprinkled some on the amma's face and gave her a little to drink from the bottle.

The amma looked at her and then pointed to the little boy, 'Feed him English food.' She drifted off to sleep. Kamala stood up. What should she do now? The boy was watching her, but he did not look scared anymore. Kamala knew only a few English words.

'Good morning, thank you, missi,' she said, and the boy burst out laughing. Kamala felt a bit annoyed. 'You are a silly crybaby,' she said in Hindi.

'I am not. You are a silly girl,' he replied in Hindi.

They watched each other suspiciously. Suddenly the boy's stomach gave a loud growl and he grinned sheepishly. He said, 'My name is Edward. I am hungry.'

'My name is Kamala. I am hungry too. Where is the food in your house?'

'I do not know.'

'Where do you eat?'

'Here, at the dining table.'

'Where is the food cooked?'

'I do not know.'

'You are a ninny.'

'I am not. I am an English boy. My father is a big sahib. You must obey me.'

'I will not.'

Kamala was a bit worried now about speaking to the boy like this. Baba would be angry, but the boy was so irritating. She was feeling very hungry too. She had had only two rotis in the morning. So much had happened since then.

'Come, we will go and look for something to eat,' she said and began walking towards the other room. The boy followed her. Then suddenly she heard a soft scraping noise in the verandah. 'Come away from the door!' she shouted and both of them ducked under the table.

'Abba, Abba.'

Kamala quickly crawled out from under the table. It was Amir. He would help them find something to eat. They would be safe now. He would know what to do with the amma.

'Amir bhai…Amir bhai…we are here…,' she shouted. Then her mouth fell open when she saw him. His clothes were torn, one eye was black and swollen. There was blood all over his kurta.

'What happened to you?' she asked, her voice faint with fear.

'Where is Abba? Please tell me where is Abba,' he cried and ran towards the back of the house. There was no one there.

'I cannot find Baba too. Where have they all gone? Some bad men came and took the sahib's things away. Look, they hit the amma. Now she won't wake up.'

Amir went to the amma and tried to wake her. She opened her eyes, then shut them quickly 'My head hurts. They have looted everything. Oh God, help us.'

'Amma, you rest. I must look for Abba.'

Amir went out into the garden and Kamala followed him. 'I do not know what to do. There is fighting everywhere in the streets. People have gone mad. They say our country has been cut in half. My friend Babloo told me to run away and hide. When I asked him why he said, "I do not know, but just hide. My uncle has taken an axe and gone out. He is shouting "Go to Pakistan or die." Babloo's uncle was so friendly. He taught me how to ride a bicycle just last month. And now he wants to hurt me.' Amir began to cry quietly. 'I don't know where my Abba is.'

Kamala could not believe this brave, bold boy, who made them all laugh, was crying. 'Come, I will wash the cut on your hand and put haldi on it. We must find some food in this house for the little boy.' The amma was now sitting up. Kamala gave her some more water to drink and then helped her lie down once more. 'Go to the kitchen, girl. There will be some food,' she murmured. Kamala found a jug of milk and some potatoes but no haldi. So she just washed Amir's hand with soap. Then she boiled the potatoes and sprinkled salt and pepper on them. Edward, Amir and she sat on the floor and ate them hot. The amma took only a sip of milk. 'Just like a picnic,' said Edward and smiled happily.

Amir looked at Kamala but did not say anything. Kamala understood that things were very bad outside the gate. They could hear people shouting in the distance and then a few gunshots would startle them. From the window they could see smoke rising on the horizon.

'They are killing each other. Just yesterday we were all friends. Why this sudden madness?' The amma folded her hands in prayer. Kamala knelt beside her and bowed her head. Amir did the same. Edward looked at them in surprise and then came and sat with them. Together they formed a tiny circle. They asked for help from different gods and the air in the room suddenly seemed charged with a brilliant light. 'Let this madness be over, let everyone be safe and let them return home soon,' they all said together.

~

For five days they lived in the house without venturing out. Kamala and Amir found some potatoes and spinach in the back garden. They boiled them and ate them with salt. Edward did not like it at first, but then he was too hungry to complain. The amma was better now but moving very slowly. She found some flour and oil in the storeroom and Amir made puris for them. There was only enough for one each. Edward began to cry for more so Amir gave him his portion. Kamala gave Amir half of her puri. The amma gave half of hers to Kamala and they all began to laugh.

But then Amir said with a worried look, 'The food will soon run out. What shall we do? I think I will go out tomorrow.'

'No, son, it is not safe. They will attack you. You are safe here because the ruffians have already been and will not come here again,' cried the amma.

But Amir would not listen.

'I must go and find Abba and also get something for you all to eat. Otherwise we will starve to death.'

Kamala watched him go out at dusk and her heart was filled with fear once more. Baba had gone and not come back. Sahib and Amir's Abba had disappeared too. Now Amir was going. What if he did not return?

Why had the world changed like this suddenly? Who had spoiled their peaceful lives? For two days Kamala sat near the window. She dared not go out into the verandah in case someone saw her. There were just a few potatoes and some radish left in the backyard. Edward was looking very pale and Kamala was so hungry that she almost ate a candle that morning.

Suddenly there was a great uproar near the gate. Kamala ran and hid behind the curtain. Someone was coming in. A big car drove in through the gate. There were men inside with guns.

'Edward, hide…hurry hide…they are here! The bad men, they will kill us!' she shouted and pushed Edward through the door to the storeroom. They huddled in there since it was the nearest room and bolted the door from inside. Edward began to cry and Kamala put her hand over his mouth. She hugged him tightly and her tears fell on his head. The amma was upstairs. What if they got her? Then someone banged loudly on the door and Kamala began to feel dizzy with fright. But Edward was crying loudly now, 'Papa we are here, Papa….'

Kamala listened. It was the sahib. She quickly unbolted the door and they both tumbled out.

'Oh, you are safe, thank God,' said the sahib. He had a bandage around his head.

Kamala was too scared to speak. Then she saw Baba. She ran to him and burst into tears. 'We are so hungry, Papa. Have you brought me some toffees?' sobbed Edward. Kamala heard Amir laugh. Everything would be all right now.

After a meal of rice and dal, rotis and four bananas, they heard each other's stories. Amir had walked in the dark to the end of Setpur town, making sure no one saw him. He found Baba lying in a ditch. His Abba was lying nearby, his head broken, his arms slashed with a knife. 'I tried to protect him. But could not. There were too many of them,' said Baba shaking his head sadly.

Amir carried them one by one to the hospital. There he found the sahib lying unconscious. Someone had hit him with a stone when he tried to stop a street fight. They left Abba at the hospital and came back to the house in a police jeep with guards.

It took three months for everyone to recover from their wounds. Sahib and Edward left for their home across the seas. Amir and his Abba went to another town. The amma went away to her village. Only Kamala and Baba remained in the house for a while. Then they too left for their village in the mountains. They never saw the others again. But none of them ever forgot the bond they had shared during those seven terrible days. Whenever Kamala dug potatoes from the fields, she took them out one by one and said, 'This one is for Amir, this one for Edward, this one for Amma and this one is for me.'

12

The Child-thief

They taught me to steal when I was six years old.

'She is the right size now,' said my father one morning, staring at me like a butcher, assessing whether the goat he was about to slaughter was the right weight or not. My mother nodded without looking up.

It was a moonless night as my father and I walked through the silent streets of a rich neighbourhood, far away from the slums where we lived. The gardens had brightly painted children's swings and big blue tubs filled with water with yellow, plastic ducks floating in them. Some gardens even had little houses for their dogs and I was imagining what kind of food these dogs ate when I was startled by my father jabbing me in the arm. The street lamps cast a yellow light on his face, changing his features and making him suddenly look like a stranger to me. He pointed to a house a little ahead of us. We started walking faster now. The street lamp was not lit outside the house. The high iron gate was shut, but the wall that encircled the house had a narrow crack which was easy for us to scale. We jumped into the garden, falling on the dew-drenched grass on silent, naked feet. We stood frozen for a few seconds. I had been trained to stand still without breathing from the time I was two years old. My mother had made me balance on the edge of the wall outside our shed and slapped me hard if I fell. I learnt very quickly to stay absolutely still. You just had to hold your breath.

The grass felt soft under my bare feet. No dogs barked. No guard shouted. My father had done his homework well. There was a large balcony covered with flowering creepers and below it, a tiny barred window.

'Go. Go in quietly and then open the door for me,' whispered my father as he gently pushed me through the window. I was a thin child with long arms. I was the perfect shape for a thief, my mother often said when she bathed me. I slipped in through the bars, wriggling like an eel and when my bare feet touched the cold floor, I waited. 'Wait till your eyes can see in the dark,' my father had said to me. Everyone at home had been very excited about my first outing as a thief. My mother had plaited my hair and tied on a new ribbon. She made jaggery sweets and fed me with her hands.

The room was silent and totally dark, but the tables and chairs seem to glisten with a hidden light. There were silver ornaments everywhere, winking at me. I held my breath and then when my eyes could see properly, I stepped forward. The door was on the far end of the room and it seemed to get further away as I walked towards it. My heart was hitting my chest so hard that I felt it would burst out of my body. My knees began trembling and I fell on the floor. I began to crawl on my hands and feet. I crawled slowly, but my heart was racing as if I was running. 'You are a snake, creeping in the grass. No one can see you or hear you,' I said to myself. My breathing calmed. The bolt on the door slid down almost on its own and in a flash of a second, my father was in the room. I had done my task.

Soon, I was the best thief in my family. I had to be, otherwise we would starve. My father now lay in bed, drunk all the time My mother had had a miscarriage and died. The baby had died too. Just as well, since there was hardly any food in the house now.

We were hungry all the time and often I had to scavenge around for scraps on the streets. My father only wanted a bottle of hooch that was brewed by one of the women in our slum colony. I did chores for her and she gave me a bottle every two or three days that kept my father happy.

When my brother Shyam turned fourteen, life became easier. He joined a gang that worked in the parking lot, stealing mobile phones and any other stuff people left in their cars. Soon he was almost as good at thieving as I was.

'You will be surprised to see how many expensive things people leave in their cars. Sometimes we don't even have to break open the car window. They leave it open for us. It is as if they want us to take all these things away from them so that they can buy more,' he laughed.

'Can I come with you one day?' I asked. Those days I was doing the rounds of the crowded markets, stealing bags, phones and anything else my nimble fingers could pick up. I later sold them to a man who specialized in handling stolen goods. I took care not to work in the same markets more than once or twice in case someone recognized me. I am a very pretty girl.

'Not a good thing for a thief to have a beautiful face,' grumbled my brother, so I often put black spots on my face to look ugly. So far I had never been caught.

But now I wanted to steal something really big that would feed us for a few months and then I could rest for a while. When I saw young girls of my age roaming around with friends, chatting and laughing, I felt so jealous. I brushed past them and swiped something from their bags. These silly little things never fetched any money but it made me feel better.

'You can come with us tomorrow, Pinky. I have cleared it with it with Boss-bhai,' said my brother.

The Boss-bhai was a lame man who lived next door to us. When I was a child he had pinched my cheeks with his twisted fingers and left a bruise. He always stared at me when I walked past and I could feel his half-closed eyes piercing my skin like needles.

'You must stay very quiet if the cops appear. Remember, they will not do anything to us since Boss-bhai pays them regularly every week,' said Shyam.

'Have you ever seen me cry, you idiot?' I said and gave him a gentle slap on his head.

It was late evening when we walked into the underground parking lot of the new shopping mall not far from our slums. A well-dressed young couple came out of the lift, loaded with shopping bags, talking in excited voices. 'I got those Nike shoes for only five thousand. Did you see the new Apple watch? Too expensive. I am glad I got the Fitbit instead.'

'I found a lovely new lipstick shade. Look—honey rust,' said the girl.

I could smell the scent on the girl's skin. Her hands looked so soft and each of her fingernails was painted a different colour. I wondered if anyone had ever hit her. They did not notice us. We were dressed in our best clothes—our working clothes—and looked almost as smart as them. Boss-bhai was sitting in his van in the parking lot. Though he was far away, I could feel his eyes watching me.

We followed the shoppers right to their car. My brother suddenly pretended to trip and fell against the boy. As the boy turned around to help him, I picked the wallet from his pocket and took his new Fitbit. They waved to us as they drove away. Fools.

Then we saw another couple walking past. Our prey. We were going to try a new trick. It needed two people to make it work.

We began to follow them. They were arguing with each other loudly and the woman kept swinging her handbag in an agitated way.

'Perfect. Fight on, my lovelies,' said my brother. We waited until the couple reached their car and got in, still arguing. As the man started the car, the woman threw all her shopping bags into the back seat. Then she threw her handbag too. Nice.

I moved forward.

'Sir…madam, excuse me, I think you have dropped something,' I said in my polite, smooth voice. I had learnt to speak like this from watching TV.

The man, startled, stared at me. I pointed to the floor. Five one hundred rupee notes were scattered on the dirty, cement floor.

'Oh! No! You stupid woman! Look!' yelled the man as he got out of the car. The woman hesitated. We held our breath. Come on, I willed her. Then she came out too.

'What are you shouting about?' she said, still angry.

The man, his wife and I all looked at the notes lying on the ground. 'You must have dropped this from your bag, madam,' I said.

'You are so careless,' said her husband.

'How are you so sure that I dropped the money?' she retorted. 'It could have fallen from your back pocket. You are forever scratching your bum,' she muttered.

I bent down and picked up the notes. They were wet and muddy. Our hard-earned money. But we had had to use the notes as bait.

The woman moved back but the man took the notes from me. Then they got into the car and drove away, arguing loudly. Shyam and I ran to the van. Boss-bhai took the shopping bags, the handbag and all the other stuff Shyam had lifted from the back seat of the car. We drove away.

Shyam and I sauntered back to the mall for a well-earned ice cream. Boss-bhai would give us our cut later on. He was a great miser and we had to often beg him for the money that was rightfully ours. We had earned it while he just sat in the van, whistling and staring at me.

That is when I got the idea. 'Why not do this on our own? We do all the work. Why should he get a share?' I asked.

'He knows how to get rid of the stolen stuff.'

'We can do it too.'

'Pinky, I don't want to take the risk.'

'We do take the risk. He just sits in the car.'

We went to the mall again the next day. I played the same trick on an elderly couple. They took so long to understand what I was saying that I almost gave up but finally, the old man came out of the car to pick up the notes I had scattered on the parking lot floor.

'Maybe they belong to someone else. We should check with the security guard,' he said and my heart sank. An honest person really makes it difficult for us to play this trick. We need greed to make it work. I waited.

'You must have dropped them,' said his wife, looking sadly at the old man.

While I talked to the old couple, my brother slipped into the car and took out the shopping bags. He only had a few minutes but he was fast. He ran with the stuff to the van, threw it in and then we walked away quickly. Boss-bhai was starting the van when the cops arrived. He ignored them. But these were not Boss-bhai's pet cops that he had bribed. These were new women cops I had called on my phone. They took Boss-bhai away in handcuffs. At least, I was free of his hateful eyes.

I am the boss now. I will steal hard. When I have enough money, my brother and I will stop. We will become ordinary people.

One day we will forget we were thieves once.

13

The Pink Velvet Dressing Gown

Nobody is sure when the dressing gown first came into the family. I always thought that it belonged to my grandmother, but my mother said it was her eldest aunt's—a present from her nephew, a black sheep who had emigrated to Canada and married a blond woman five years older than him. The aunt never wore it because she was sure the mem had chosen it. Moreover, it was a lurid shade of pink and her husband thought it would make her look like a woman of the bazaar. 'Which bazaar woman ever wears a dressing gown?' asked my mother's aunt and my mother wondered how my uncle knew about such things.

After keeping it wrapped in its original gold-embossed white plastic bag for a year, the aunt finally gave the dressing gown to my mother.

'What a stupid gift to send. She could never have worn it. The nephew must have gone mad after marrying that woman,' my mother grumbled every time she saw the dressing gown. The aunt, an energetic eighty-year-old lady could have never worn any dressing gown because women of her generation went to bed fully dressed in a sari, blouse and petticoat and only undressed while bathing. My mother never really used the dressing gown either, only wearing it on special occasions when unexpected visitors dropped by early in the morning before she had had her bath.

The dressing gown had a frilled collar edged with gold lace and as the years went by, the cruel Indian heat began to affect the velvet fabric, making it shrivel up around the edges. But the collar still held itself upright like a chameleon's ruffle, around my mother's cascading grey curls. My father said it made her look like Louis XIV, especially when she stood on the balcony quarrelling and bargaining with the vegetable hawker below on the street. Beggars passing by would often call out to her, 'O Queen, throw us a coin.' She tried to give the gown away to various relatives who came to visit, but nobody would have it even though it was 'imported' and quite expensive. Years passed and the dressing gown began to look different. The soft pink gradually acquired a brownish glow like Europeans who have lived under the Indian sun for many years. The pink velvet changed its soft texture as patches of coconut hair oil, sandalwood talcum powder and Tiger 'headache' balm stained it with a pale gold patina, and the golden lace turned coppery with age.

Finally, my mother gave the dressing gown to me when I was in hospital having my first child. 'You can wrap the baby in it if it is a girl.' My mother-in-law did not want me to wear the dressing gown because she was worried it would tempt the gods to send us a female child instead of the much longed for son. When my daughter was born, I did not wrap her in the dressing gown because she was underweight and had to be kept inside an incubator. My mother knitted her a tiny pink blanket overnight and we would watch her through the glass panes as she slept curled up like a pink caterpillar. I wore the dressing gown while breastfeeding my daughter and the sweet smell of milk now mingled with the heady aroma of oil, talcum powder and balm; though the gown was washed often it still retained its strange smell which my dog loved. She would curl up on the dressing gown at night and if I tried to pull it away she would growl softly. As she grew old, clumps of her grey and white fur began to cling to the balding velvet.

I have worn the dressing gown for many winters now and every time I try half-heartedly to discard it, my daughter protests. 'You will look like someone else if you get another dressing gown.' My husband too likes its faded pale colour, and when I bring it out to wear on the first chilly morning of winter, he always says, 'Winter is here.' My son, though fastidious about everything else, still loves its soft mouldy texture and when he was a child, he would cling to the trailing belt with both hands and skate behind me as I walked around the house.

Though the pink colour has disappeared mostly, a small bright patch under the collar remains to remind me of the original brazen pink so hated by my great-uncle. The gold lace too has long vanished and the frilly collar no longer stands regally upright like it used to. Instead it flops, tired and spent around my shoulders.

Every year when winter is over, I pack the dressing gown in a trunk along with other warm clothes in a layer of margosa leaves to protect them from insects. Before I place the gown amongst the bright new sweaters and shawls, I touch the torn pocket which my children had tugged while playing hide-and-seek behind me. I gather the fragile velvet and hold it against my face. I inhale its strange fragrance of milk, talcum powder, balm, dog fur and hair oil. I smell my mother in it. I wrap the sleeves around my neck and the faded velvet is now dull brown like my skin. I have to keep it forever.

14

Roses for My Love

Mr Sen, still handsome and fit in his seventh decade and incredibly vain, liked women who were plump and a bit silly in a sweet, innocent way. His wife, to his regret, was as slim as a gymnast in training with a Ph.D. in botany.

He had only met her once before they had got married fifty years ago; a brief 'viewing' at her palatial house, surrounded by her noisy uncles and aunts who had not let her speak a single word to him. If he had known how clever she was, how highly educated, he might have rejected the match.

His own family sat stunned, sipping tea, overawed by the girl's wealth, status in society and the huge, impressive house. His parents had been surprised when the offer for this match had come from a distant relative who knew both parties—surprised and delighted since they were much lower down in the social ladder and not as rich, so his father had quickly agreed to the match after the first meeting before he, the prospective bridegroom, could say anything. Not that he was asked. 'Did you see the white marble staircase leading to the first floor? I have only seen something like that in films,' his mother had gushed, her eyes sparkling with glee.

'She is plain-looking but an only child and will inherit the house. Well done, son,' his father had said proudly.

'I knew good fortune awaited him ever since he won the first prize in the "Cutest Baby" contest,' his mother had said, patting his head as if he was still a baby. They had both looked at him with satisfied smiles. He had finally won their approval though he had done nothing at all except win a prize in the marriage market.

'Fifty years have flown past so quickly,' thought Mr Sen as he came out of the house. Dawn was breaking slowly and a fine mist hung over the trees in the garden. He walked towards a wooden bench and sat down near the rose bushes. He very seldom sat here, but today he needed to clear his aching head, which felt as if it was stuffed with lead. The servant boy was staring at him in a frightened sort of way and he ordered him to go away and leave him alone. 'At your age you should not drink so much. You need to be careful,' he was sure his wife would say as soon as she saw him in this sorry state. He looked up at her bedroom windows which were still shut and hoped she would not wake up too early. The party last night had been for their wedding anniversary. He had forgotten to get a gift for her. Anyway, he had no idea what she would like. They hardly ever exchanged presents now.

'Fifty years is a lifetime,' thought Mr Sen as he sat nursing his aching head and staring at the roses his wife loved so much. He often said to their friends that his wife cared more about her precious roses than him and she always replied 'I certainly do', but with a gentle smile which never failed to please him.

The weak sunlight now streaming through the garden was hurting his eyes and he shut them. He could hear his phone ringing but he had left it in his bedroom and he felt too tired to go and fetch it. He would ask the servant later to bring it down. Who could be calling him so early in the morning? Maybe it was their son, who lived nearby though they hardly ever saw him since he was a busy, successful doctor.

A crow suddenly cawed above his head, its call harsh and strident and Mr Sen opened his eyes reluctantly. His wife's roses were now sparkling in the sunshine and then he saw her coming out of the house. Mr Sen shifted uncomfortably in his chair, waiting for Rita to reprimand him in her stern, matron-like voice. He knew she worried about his health, he was seventy-eight now, but he wished she would let him have some fun.

His thoughts returned to the night before. They had had guests over for dinner, his friends from the Golf Club—a loud, raucous bunch. They drank too much, spilled wine on the carpet and refused to eat dinner till it was well past midnight. Rita had got very upset when they started making jokes about women in that crude, school-boyish way like they always did. What was the harm in a few jokes about fat women, ugly women, old women. He had found them quite amusing, idiotic, but amusing, but had sheepishly looked away when he saw Rita frowning.

'Why don't you joke about ugly, fat, old men,' she had asked, silencing his friends with a sharp look and left the room. They had slept in separate bedrooms now for many years. Rita said his snoring kept her awake and he liked having a midnight snack which also disturbed her. 'Who eats namkeen in the middle of the night, for God's sake,' she would say. She, on the other hand, read till midnight and that irritated him. 'Why can't you finish reading all your books during the day?' he would say. So now they occupied separate bedrooms on different floors of this vast house. Sometimes they did not see each other at all for the entire day except at night when they passed each other on the marble staircase which had so impressed his mother fifty years ago.

The sun dipped behind a cloud and the light changed, growing dim and grey, as Rita came and stood near him, her thin hands outstretched. She was looking at him in a strange way, as if seeing him for the first time.

'I am so happy I found you here. Have you seen my roses? See how many new buds have opened,' she said as she sat down next to him. Then she gave him a gentle nudge and pointed to the flowers just in case he had not understood what she was saying.

Relieved that she was not angry with him, Mr Sen quickly got up and walked towards the roses. He could not see any new buds but he nodded enthusiastically, pretending to admire the flowers; he could not understand what the fuss was about these roses. Rita was always discussing them with the old mali. These rose bushes needed special food, special soil, and all kinds of extra attention like a delicate child, before they produced any flowers. One flower looked very much like another flower to Mr Sen, except sometimes he noticed that they came in different colours. He preferred vegetables any day. At least they had some use. A big, white cauliflower or a large bunch of juicy, red tomatoes impressed him much more than his wife's fragile, forever demanding roses.

'Shall we go for a stroll around the garden?' asked Rita, her voice soft and low. Mr Sen was not keen but his wife looked at him in such an appealing way, that he could not refuse.

It was so rare for his wife to ask him to do anything. She was amazingly capable and efficient and looked after him and the huge house with meticulous care as if she was running a company. She made sure he took his medicines on time, got the servants to arrange his clothes exactly the way he liked, ordered only the dishes he wanted to eat and made sure everything ran smoothly. He did not have to do a thing except occasionally sign a cheque.

How he longed for a wife who was helpless and looked at him with pleading eyes, like a puppy asking for treats. But this morning, Rita's eyes, usually stern and unforgiving, had a girlish, innocent look he had never seen before.

He must have done something right last evening to please his wife but that was impossible. Mr Sen tried desperately to think back but everything seemed so blurred. He knew he had had too much to drink and the last thing he could remember, was shouting and waving to his friends as they stumbled out of the house. Then he had passed out. When he woke up, he had found himself sprawled on the carpet in the study with his shoes still on. The servants had not helped him up to his bedroom as they usually did after a drinking binge. In fact, he had noticed the house seemed strangely quiet before staggering up to his bedroom and going back to sleep again. His phone kept ringing but he ignored it and fell into a deep, whisky-induced stupor.

Mr Sen shot a worried glance at his wife but Rita did not seem angry at all as she walked with him in the garden. Her face wore a calm, serene look and she kept smiling. It was years since they had walked like this together and he was surprised to find how much it pleased him. He tried to reach out and hold her hand but she slipped away.

'It will rain later today. The sky is already turning grey. Can you see the clouds gathering above the house?' whispered Rita. 'You must tell the mali not to water the roses tomorrow,' she said.

'Why? Where are you going tomorrow?' he asked, not really interested. They both had their own routines and neither asked the other what was going on in their lives. Had it always been like this? Had there been a time when they had talked to each other? Had asked each other questions and listened to the answers? he thought as he looked at his wife.

Fifty years was a long time ago and Mr Sen could not even remember what he had had for lunch yesterday.

'Happy anniversary,' he said, feeling a bit embarrassed and shy, but Rita did not seem to have heard him. She pointed to the roses again, her pale hands trembling for some reason. Had she always been so fragile-looking ?

'Make sure the mali comes every day. He is a bit lazy and gives all kinds of excuses for not turning up. You can ask Din Bahadur to keep an eye on him. Please do not forget to give him extra money for his son's tuition fees,' she said, turning her face towards him. 'Remember the day we employed Din Bahadur? We both had no idea what to ask him to do. We were so young and foolish, at least I was,' he said, laughing awkwardly.

Mr Sen was surprised to hear her laughing too. 'You were. I always found that so endearing about you,' she said. Suddenly they were both transported back fifty years. They had laughed and talked to each other so much then. He remembered teaching her how to drive. She had learnt in just two days and he was a bit disappointed. He was hoping to carry on the lessons for weeks. It made him feel so good to be able to share something with his clever wife, to be in control.

He had realized very soon after their marriage, with a twinge of regret, that Rita was exceptionally bright. Whenever he tried to tell her something, she already knew about it. Politics, science, arts and literature—she knew so much about everything much to his irritation. The only thing she had no idea about was golf but then she did not care about it. Mr Sen tried to keep up with her at first, reading the newspaper from cover to cover every morning so that he could discuss politics with her, but he seemed to get many of the facts wrong and though she corrected him politely, it made him feel so foolish. He even bought a general knowledge book to learn up facts about history and literature but he soon gave up. It was too exhausting. He wished he had a wife who talked about ordinary things like food, servants and shopping and was not a resident teacher who was assessing him all the time and finding him lacking.

All that was a long time ago. They had lived together now for years in a detached yet friendly way with occasional arguments about petty things which he always lost, but she was a good wife to him and he could not complain. Had she ever felt lonely, he wondered for the first time; had she longed for a husband who was as smart and as highly educated as her? Anyway, it was too late for both of them. Maybe in their next life they would choose more suitable partners? For some reason that thought did not make him happy and Mr Sen tried to walk closer to his wife, but she seemed to have moved away.

'I remember how you tried to boil an egg and it was raw when we cracked it open,' said Mr Sen, looking at his wife, hoping to make her laugh again.

'I was hopeless at cooking,' she agreed.

'You were, but you are so good at everything else,' said Mr Sen.

'I tried, you know. I even went to cooking classes but could never learn. Anyway you preferred Din Bahadur's fiery curries to my insipid food. Though my bland food is better for your health, but no more nagging today,' she said.

Mr Sen shook his head but said nothing. He was still a bit surprised at how much they were talking to each other today. It was almost as if the five decades had never happened and they were a young married couple again. Rita's face had a strange glow this morning, as if the gentle sunlight had erased the passing years and she was a bride again. She was not pretty or plump and certainly not silly and Mr Sen had come to respect her over the years.

He looked at her again and suddenly realized that he loved her in a strange, mysterious way that he himself could not understand. Why had he never told her that? Maybe he always felt too shy and hesitant, too much in awe of her. He reached his hand out to touch her; to tell her he loved her, but then the light changed in the garden and the trees began to sway as if a storm was approaching and Rita moved away silently.

'Wait!' Mr Sen called out to his wife, but she had disappeared into the shadows beyond the rose bushes and he was suddenly alone in the garden.

'I will tell her later. I must,' he said, looking at his wife's precious roses, startled by their beauty and their intense colour, which he had never noticed before.

Suddenly, he heard a sound and looked around. He saw his son walking towards him. He seemed so weary and tired. A wave of fear flooded over Mr Sen, his heart began to race and he knew what his son was going to say even before he spoke the terrible words.

'Ma has gone. We tried very hard, but her heart gave way early this morning. I have been trying to call you for hours,' he said, as he sank into the chair, sobbing.

Mr Sen stood very still, his heart shattering into pieces with grief. A sweet, delicate scent drifted up from the roses towards him as the wind rushed through the garden. Tears flowed down his face, blinding him, but he knew she was still with him, his clever, beloved wife.

15

A Murder in the Wedding Season

The old house, perched on a steep hillside, groaned under the weight of two dozen relatives. Soni had stopped counting after the twentieth aunt arrived at the gate, sweaty and tired, asking for change for her rickshaw fare. Soni had hoped that the landslides caused by the recent rains would deter some of the relatives who lived further afield, but not a single one had regretted the invitation to the wedding.

'Rai Bahadur Daulatji's granddaughter's wedding—no landslides can keep us away,' an uncle aged eighty-one had written, and arrived with his catheter in tow.

'Your late husband will be sad if we don't come. His soul will weep in sorrow when he looks down from heaven and sees we are not there,' said an aunt and landed up with her four unmarried daughters. Soni had planned for eight or ten people staying in her four-and-a-half bedroom house in Shimla but now it seemed there were bodies everywhere.

Suitcases were piled high behind tables and every available surface had a bedding roll spread out. The good thing was that no one needed looking after. Various aunts took charge of the kitchen while the uncles and nephews dealt with the tent-wallah, keeping a watchful eye on the quality of crockery, the freshness of marigold garlands, and the sturdiness of the hired aluminum chairs. Soni felt quite superfluous at times and ran away to hide in her bedroom, occupied, thankfully, only by her daughter Mita, the bride to be, and her.

Soni had agreed somewhat reluctantly to this match. She was unhappy about her daughter marrying a boy from such an old-fashioned, wealthy family. Rohit was a well-mannered, intelligent boy and Soni liked him but she was nervous about Mita, so outspoken and wilful, fitting into a traditional joint family. Rohit's grandfather owned sugar mills and had vast acres of land in Uttar Pradesh where they lived in a huge mansion built in what Rohit jokingly called 'new feudal style'. Rohit's father was a well-known politician and his uncle was the local MLA.

'Rohit is a wonderful boy but his family—they are not like us,' Soni had said once to Mita but her daughter had replied, laughing, 'Ma, no one is like us. We are a unique family. Papa was a famous scientist but totally eccentric, you are unlike any other mother I know, and Bobby is a child prodigy. Even our dogs are odd. Rohit's family is filthy rich but very ordinary and very boring.'

Soni looked at her late husband's photograph on her bedside table and asked him once again, 'Do you approve? Is Mita doing the right thing?' His kind face looked at her, the black and white image as impassive as it had been in real life. His gentle, absent-minded eyes smiled at her. 'Do what you think is right, Soni,' she heard him say, in his 'don't bother me voice'.

~

'The knees are fine but my digestion is really bad,' said Banno Bua, rubbing her stomach gently to demonstrate. She was around fifty-five but behaved like a much older woman, keeping her head covered with her white lace-edged dupatta all the time. But her face was still beautiful and her large brown eyes darted about restlessly as if she was always looking for something she had lost. Banno Bua had a strong, melodious voice and was much in demand at weddings for her repertoire of old folk songs. Soni was not sure how the old lady was related to them, but she liked her best amongst all the relatives who had come to attend Mita's wedding. Banno Bua helped with the chores quietly and never offered endless advice like the other aunts and uncles. She even helped Bobby with his school project quite happily.

Soni had once heard her sing a very naughty song but in a soft, mocking voice which others could not hear.

'I went to fetch water from the well, dear friend, but my brother-in-law caught me by the wrist…then by the elbow, then by the ankle…,' she sang, laughing to herself, and suddenly Soni caught a glimpse of the girl she must have once been in that elderly woman's face.

'Don't tell anyone I sang this one,' she whispered to Soni, her eyes sparkling. Soni knew that Banno Bua had been widowed at a very young age and had probably had to learn to behave like all the older widows of the family. She must have trained herself to act like an elderly, sedate woman years ago, when she was still young. She must have erased her real self, bit by bit, to blend in with the family, till she forgot she was ever a carefree young woman.

Mita and Soni urged her one day to wear a colourful sari and a pair of pretty pearl earrings but Banno Bua shook her head.

'Never. Not safe for widows to look like parakeets. White protects us,' she said, giving them a blank, faraway look.

~

Now there were just three days left for the wedding and Soni finally discarded her anxiety and began to bask in the infectious, joyous spirit swirling around her old house. Every evening, Banno Bua sang late into the night, charming everyone with her honeyed voice, and all the women gathered around her to form a chorus of discordant but happy voices. That evening she was singing a song about a docile new bride and her mean mother-in-law when she suddenly stopped.

'Who is that man, Soni, staring at us from the balcony?' she whispered, beating the dholki loudly to drown her voice.

'He claims he is a friend of my late father-in-law's and he's also Rohit's granduncle. He wants to stay with us instead of the hotel the boy's side had booked for him. 'More fun with the girl's side,' he had said. I couldn't refuse, even though it meant giving him a whole room to himself, so inconvenient when we're so cramped for space,' Soni replied. 'He used to be an actor, they say. He is an MLA now.' For some reason she couldn't quite fathom, she did not like the look of this man who was smiling down at them, waving a red handkerchief. Gold rings studded with different-coloured stones flashed on each of his fat fingers. His face had a deep scar on one cheek and his dyed black hair had white patches, making him look like an old raccoon. He laughed and began swaying to the music, snapping his fingers, staring at the young girls.

Banno Bua finished her song abruptly and put the drum away despite everyone's protests. 'I am tired, I am going to bed,' she said and hurried away. Soni wondered what had upset her but then she forgot all about her. The singing went on for a long time and some of the children fell asleep on the carpet, clinging to their mothers' saris, while one very old uncle snored on the sofa, clutching his false teeth in his hands.

The singing finally ended and the guests drifted away, walking unsteadily with sleep-blind eyes to their various corners and crawled into their makeshift beds. Night crept into the old house and now shadows swayed languidly on the walls, as if still continuing the merry singing and dancing. A fine mist covered the garden, touching the trees with damp, cold hands and the moon hid behind the mountains as if it was sulking. There was a strange, whining sound as the wind rattled the windows of the house and knocked on the doors, as though someone was trying to get in.

Soni opened her eyes with a start. Something had woken her up. Then she heard the noise again and jumped up from the bed. She went to the door and listened but she could not hear anything now. 'Must be the prawns you ate at dinner, giving you nightmares. Go back to sleep, Ma,' mumbled Mita sleepily.

Soni could not go back to sleep so she got up and went down to the kitchen, tripping over someone sleeping on the floor in the corridor. Then she saw it was only a quilt and a discarded pillow. Someone was awake and walking around the house.

She wondered absent-mindedly who it was as she went into the kitchen to make herself a cup of tea. Then she went out into the verandah. The hills were still draped in a thick grey mist. It was almost dawn and the trees in the garden were touched by circles of grey-gold light. Later, Soni would remember that the birds were uncharacteristically quiet that dawn.

~

It was the tent-wallah's assistant who found the body when he was arranging the lights. He was perched on the top step of a ladder propped against the wall, draping the wires through the bars of a window in one of the upstairs bedrooms, and that is when he saw a body lying twisted at an odd angle on the carpet, next to the bed inside the room. The bed sheets were soaked in blood, and it looked as though the body had fallen off the bed. The tent-wallah's assistant almost fell off the ladder as he turned around to shout to the boys working in the lawns below.

Then there was utter chaos.

The house trembled and shook as people ran around shouting and screaming. They tried to get into the room but it was locked from inside. Then one nephew climbed up the ladder and jumped in through the window. 'Oh my God! Dead! He is dead!' the nephew shouted to all the relatives gathered outside the door and they gave a collective cry of horror. The poor nephew barely managed to unbolt the door, before they all rushed in to get a look at the corpse.

Manmohanji had been dead for at least five hours, the doctor said, shaking his head as if he could not believe it. 'He was in good health for his age. If this terrible thing had not happened he could have lived till ninety,' he said, washing his hands.

The body was carried away for a post-mortem on a stretcher, draped in a white sheet. The relatives pushed each other to get a better look and an aunt fainted when she saw the bloodstains. The women wailed and the children hid behind the doors in fear. They had forgotten to switch the music off and a melodious shehnai echoed all over the house as everyone talked in agitated, excited voices.

'He was stabbed by a thief who came to steal the wedding jewels.'

'No, no! Such a respectable man cannot be murdered. He had a heart attack, then fell down and cut his head.'

'This is a political murder. The opposition party must have sent an assassin.'

'Blood…so much blood for an old man!'

'He committed suicide. Cut his own throat!'

'That is impossible. You can cut someone else's throat but not your own. For suicide you have to cut your wrists and sit in a bathtub filled with water.'

'He died of food poisoning. Prawns are always dangerous.'

'What about the blood then?'

Everyone had an opinion. Even the children had forgotten their fears and were now running around looking for clues, led by Bobby.

The household was divided into two groups. The younger lot thought Manmohanji had been murdered and went around the house searching for clues along with the children, while the older uncles and aunts were certain he had died of a heart attack or food poisoning. They could not believe that a man from such a wealthy, important family could be murdered. Arguments and opinions filled the house. Soni's head was spinning and everything seemed like a bad dream. All she knew was that the wedding would now have to be postponed.

~

Police, press and more relatives arrived. 'Death due to unnatural causes,' said the police. Manmohanji had not died of a heart attack in his sleep as all the elder relatives had believed. He had been drugged and then his throat had been slit with a knife or some such sharp instrument. They had not found the murder weapon as yet.

'We told you so,' said the younger lot gleefully and threw themselves into a hunt for the knife.

The murderer had apparently mixed sleeping pills in the old man's bedtime Horlicks and then cut his throat. He (they all assumed it was a he) had cut the dead man's face with the knife for no reason at all.

The police called in everyone they thought was important for questioning one by one, which meant all the men in the house and the tent-wallah's assistant. They left the women out since they did not want to upset them. '…and in any case women never remember anything and make very unreliable witnesses,' said the young inspector to Soni over his third cup of tea. His name was Ramesh Sen and he had been born in the same town that Rohit's family came from. 'A great, generous man he was—our Manmohanji. Just inaugurated our new police station building and now he is lying in the morgue in the very same station. Life is very tricky,' he said, shaking his head.

The inspector asked the servants a lot of questions and for two days Soni had to send for food from a hotel nearby because the cook was too upset to prepare any meals. The police suspected an old enmity. 'Some rival gang must have been jealous of his success, either from the acting world or someone from politics. I suspect an actor; they have very fiery tempers and are very unpredictable,' said Inspector Sen. He sighed and then began telling Soni about his various health problems when he learnt that she was a Reiki teacher.

After three days of relentless questioning, the police suddenly stopped. No one came to the house anymore and Soni learnt from a journalist friend that the police had been ordered to close the case. The chief minister was very annoyed with the bad publicity since the most shocking stories were appearing in the newspapers every day about Manmohanji's past life.

'Manmohan Thakur is now a liability to the party and his name should be erased without delay from public memory,' the chief minister wrote to the inspector general of police, and the IG ordered Inspector Sen to close the case. The file was stamped CLOSED and put in the old wooden cupboard in the back room of the Shimla police station along with other ancient unsolved cases.

The wedding was postponed. The mango leaf decorations wilted and were taken down, the flowers were removed although the bamboo poles around which they had been entwined, and the wires for the lights, still remained in place, giving the house a ghostly, ruined look. An uneasy quiet descended on the place as the relatives began to leave one by one.

'Dangerous lunatic in the house. Maybe our turn next,' they muttered.

'Bad omen, better cancel this rishta totally and find a new boy,' one aunt advised before leaving.

Soni did not know whether to be relieved or sad, though Mita seemed unperturbed. 'Rohit is not too upset about his granduncle. Apparently he was quite an evil fellow. When Rohit was a child, he often punished him for no reason at all. He locked him up in the bathroom if he didn't finish his milk or forgot to brush his teeth. Even his parents were afraid of the old man. You know, Ma, he had many cases against him in their village in UP. Rohit feels someone from their village murdered him. Anyway, we can have a quiet wedding now after a few months. The old man did us a favour by popping off like this,' she said. Soni scolded Mita for speaking ill of the dead but had to admit to herself that she felt relieved.

The house was now empty of all relatives. Only Banno Bua continued to stay on with them. She said nothing about leaving, just walked around the house mumbling under her breath. 'Poor old man. He seemed quite healthy to me. But you never know what is waiting for you around the corner. Fate always has a plan for everyone,' she said to Soni, her eyes shining in a slightly mad way.

Soni was worried about Banno Bua. Why had she not left with the other relatives? What was there for her to do in the house now? Bobby was certain she was mad. She kept asking Soni endless questions.

'Why did the police inspector leave? He should have spent more time here. How did the thief come into the room? The door was locked from inside. Must have been very clever, the murderer, don't you think? It takes a lot of strength to kill such a big man.'

One evening Soni had seen her go into the room where Manmohanji had died. She seemed to be humming to herself as she moved around the room, touching the bed, the chairs, and the ornaments on the table. Soni had told the servants to lock the room after that.

'Mita, I am worried about her. Do you think this death has unhinged her mind?' asked Soni. Bobby, who was sitting with his laptop at the dining table, instantly downloaded a list of symptoms of insanity from Wikipedia, which he read out gleefully.

'Why should it make her go off the rails? She didn't even know the old man,' said Mita.

'She did ask me who he was. You know, that day when she was singing in the courtyard, but then so did so many other relatives. Punit Chacha even tried to borrow money from Manmohanji and was very angry when the old man refused. "Miser! Will he take his gold with him when he dies?" he had said to me, I remember. Poor man must be regretting it now,' Soni said.

'Why don't you talk to Banno Bua, Ma?' said Mita. 'You may not be able to cure her of her mental illness but you could at least calm her down a bit.'

'When is she leaving?' asked Rohit.

'I don't know. She has not said anything to me and I can't ask her "why are you still here?" That would be rude,' said Soni.

'Let her stay, Ma. I like her and she is harmless. All this murder business must have given her a thrill in her sad and empty life and she is making the most of it,' said Mita, and Rohit agreed.

Soni put her book down and looked out into the garden from her chair in the verandah. There were potholes in the ground where they had stuck bamboo poles and all the plants in the flower beds were badly trampled. She sighed. The garden was her pride, and it would take her a while to get it back to its former glory. Suddenly Soni saw something glittering on one of the rocks near the rose bushes. She got up and walked down the verandah steps into the garden. The sunlight was falling at an angle, making the stone on the ring glitter. Where had she seen this ring before? Soni thought as she bent to pick it up.

She tried her best but could not remember. She walked thoughtfully back to the house, the ring in her hand. When she held it up to examine it more closely, she noticed there were dark brown spots on the gold. Could it be blood? Then she suddenly recalled Manmohanji's smiling face and the rings flashing on his fingers. She looked up and saw Banno Bua watching her from an upstairs window. She was in Manmohanji's room once more. The servants must have forgotten to lock the door that morning after they'd cleaned the room.

'Should we tell the police? I am sure it belonged to him,' Soni said to Mita, showing her the ring. She had placed it in a paper envelope since she did not want anyone else to touch it.

'Well, we should give it to them. It is evidence after all, but I think they will just pocket it. Maybe we should just give it to Rohit's father. Let him decide what to do with it,' said Mita.

'The thief must have dropped it when he was escaping. It must have fallen out of the handkerchief,' said Banno's voice suddenly, giving Soni a start. She had not seen her come up behind her. The old woman moves so silently, it's creepy, thought Soni.

'Mita, there was no handkerchief. The ring was just lying there in the mud. Why did Banno Bua say that? How odd,' Soni mused as Banno Bua moved off and went out into the garden. They could see her plucking flowers for her puja, singing softly to herself.

A strange thought was running through Soni's head as she shut her eyes and went back to that horrible night. She had been woken by someone groaning though she had never told the inspector about it. Maybe she should have. Soni tried to think about that night. What had she done? Yes, she had gone downstairs to the kitchen. She had seen something on the kitchen table that had not seemed right. What was it? She had noticed it at that time and said to herself, 'How odd! That should not be there.'

But what was it? She just could not remember and felt irritated with herself.

The next day the mali found a red handkerchief in the rocky hollow below the pine tree at the far end of the garden. There was another ring in the muddy bundle. 'The police did not see this because it was under a fallen tree trunk. They were too lazy to search under the rocks,' said the mali proudly, handing over the red bundle to her. 'Do I get a reward? There must be a reward from the government,' he said, his eyes shining greedily. Soni gave him five hundred rupees though Mita said she should have given him more since he could have easily kept the gold ring.

Mita was obviously right because later she heard the mali mutter, 'Honesty never pays nowadays.'

How did Banno Bua know about the red handkerchief? Was she hiding something from them? The police had not questioned her at all though she always stood by the door when Inspector Sen was there. 'I must talk to her. Even if it's unpleasant. At any rate I must confront her soon and find out what her plans are,' said Soni to herself.

'We don't know anything about her,' Soni thought as she lay in bed that night. Something about Banno Bua bothered her now. She had seemed a simple, kind woman—a bit lonely—but now there was something furtive and secretive about her which she had not noticed before. What was going on in her mind?

Then Soni had an idea. She would go down to the kitchen, retracing her steps. Then she would remember what had been odd about the kitchen table that night. She often did that to jolt her memory into recalling things.

Soni opened the door silently and crept down the dark corridor. A faint flickering light shone through from the street light outside. Shimla still had the old lamps from British days that were struggling on bravely. Soni could not see anything in the kitchen so she made her way to the bedroom where Manmohanji had stayed. Where he had died. It had remained unoccupied since then because nobody wanted to sleep there but tonight the door was open. The servants must have forgotten to lock the door again. Soni put her hand out to switch on the light and suddenly a soft hand touched her fingers. Soni froze in terror. There was a figure draped in white behind the door. Soni opened her mouth to scream and then she heard the soft voice. It was Banno Bua.

'I have come to pick up my dupatta. I left it somewhere here,' she said. In a flash Soni remembered what it was that she had seen that night on the kitchen table. It was Banno Bua's white dupatta and it had red stains on it.

Soni opened her mouth to speak, but Banno put her fingers on her lips. 'I know. You can see it all. I am a wicked woman and I have blood on my clothes. I will always have blood on my clothes,' she said, looking beyond into the dark garden.

She remembered his cold eyes, his smiling face looming over her. She remembered his laughter, her screams, the blood on her clothes, the gold rings on his fingers. 'You are a wicked girl, I knew it as soon as I set eyes on you. A shameless wicked girl!' he had said to her later as she lay sobbing on the floor. The shame burnt her entire being and she felt herself torn into shreds. Her body twisted with pain as she curled herself tightly into a knot, like an animal about to die.

'Soni, beti, I wish I could have worn my red wedding sari for your daughter's wedding but I am a widow and it is not allowed,' Banno Bua whispered as she pulled her dupatta over her face. The she went and touched the pillow on the bed. Manmohanji's scarf was still lying there. Banno Bua twisted it in her hands.

'Did you know him, Banno Bua?' Soni asked softly though her heart was racing with fear. She must be careful not to say anything which would push this woman over the edge.

Banno Bua recited as though in her sleep, 'He came into my bedroom three days after my husband had died. "You must be lonely, my poor girl," he said, touching my face. I was fifteen years old and afraid of him. He was my father-in-law's rich cousin. "I will take you away from here tonight. I will buy you pretty clothes. You don't have to wear white anymore," he said to me. He tore my white sari off me that night, filled my body with shame. He put scars on me that I can never erase. I have waited for a long time to find him. I just cut his throat a little bit but he bled like a pig. Stupid old man!' She gave a laugh that was more like a sob. Then she threw the scarf out of the window. 'It is not far, look. I climbed up the ladder and jumped in through the window quite easily. I may look like an old woman to you but I am still quite strong. I can twist your neck for you. But you are a kind woman and I like you, Soni beti.'

Soni watched her silently, not sure what to say, and then Banno spoke again, 'So now I can wear red at your daughter's wedding,' she said, laughing loudly and sobbing at the same time.

That night, three days before the wedding, when the moon was hiding behind the mountains, the women found Banno asleep on the cold floor in the corridor covered with just a quilt and no mattress beneath her. 'Poor woman, she is used to sleeping on the floor,' they said as they retired to the room leading off from the corridor and settled themselves comfortably on the cots and beddings that had been laid out.

Banno Bua just lay quietly smiling to herself.

They never heard the door open. They never knew what took place in the room next to theirs.

He had not cried out when she entered his room. He was so pleased that she had come to see him though he was not sure who she was.

'You are a very pretty woman. Come, come sit by me. Tell me again, when did we meet?' he had asked. The stupid fool, too vain to wear his glasses! She had simpered coyly, slipping the pills into the glass of Horlicks on his bedside table. 'Drink it up while it's hot,' she cooed to him. 'Then we can talk.' She waited while he drank the Horlicks. Then, as his eyes began to glaze over, she had told him. She had touched the scar on his face that she had made with her nails that night long ago, but by then he was already struggling to keep his eyes open. No, he had not cried out at all when she killed him, when she cut his face with her knife, which was a shame because she would have liked to hear him cry out in pain like she had done so many years ago. It was she who had cried, a long moaning wail as though letting out all the grief she had stored within her.

She shut her eyes and remembered his blood on her dupatta. Now they were even. It had taken many years but now they were even.

In the darkness, Soni saw Mita slip quietly into the room. She came and stood next to her. Banno sat on the bed and cried, her entire body shaking with each sob and in between her cries, she tried to talk to them though they could not understand most of her broken words. It seemed as if she was talking in a strange language, using words they had never heard before. But they strung together the incoherent words edged with pain and understood what had happened one night many years ago.

Then Banno fell silent at last. The three women stood by the window and watched dawn break over the mountains and the sky paint itself a new colour once more. One by one, the hill crows began to call in harsh notes and then the soothing song of a lone thrush began in the garden.

Mita held Banno Bua's hand and led her away from the window. 'We will find your dupatta. You go to sleep now and everything will be all right. There is nothing to be afraid of anymore. Ma and

I will take care of you,' Mita said, speaking in a soft, soothing voice as if to a child.

Banno Bua nodded and smiled. She would wear her red wedding sari. It was in her suitcase along with the knife she always carried with her, hoping to meet him one day. She would keep the knife forever because she might meet him in another life.

She would love to kill him once again.

16

The Invisible Child

At first she felt a slight tingling sensation on the back of her neck. Maya ignored it and continued to read her book, adjusting the table lamp so that the light would fall directly on the page and not create pools of shadows around her. She could hear the sound of rain become louder and suddenly the room was ablaze with silver light. She looked out of the window and saw a giant streak of lightning crackle and split into a million fragments of tiny lights as it raced across the sky. For a few moments, the entire hillside was lit up in a brilliant white and gold light and then swiftly, darkness swooped down again.

'There is sure to be a massive landslide tomorrow. My path will be cut off again but what does it matter,' thought Maya as she turned the pages of her book. It was an exciting novel with a complicated plot and she wanted to finish it before going to bed. The electricity always went out when there was a thunderstorm and Maya did not want to read in candlelight since she was afraid of setting her old wooden house on fire. 'I must remember to get the emergency light fixed,' she told herself sternly, knowing very well that she would soon forget about it again.

The rain was now drumming noisily over the slate roof of the house and pouring down the stained, cracked windowpanes. It sounded as if a crowd of desperate people was running on her roof to get somewhere urgently. Maya smiled and thought about the old, broken slate tiles bearing the weight of a hundred people. The house was old and needed urgent repairs, but she ignored the leaking roof, cracked plaster, and the mice running around. She was content to live in this decrepit, spider-filled house which had once belonged to an English family more than a hundred years ago. Nobody had wanted it so she bought it very cheaply from the local village shopkeeper. 'Not a safe place for a woman. People hear strange sounds like of a child crying and so we never go there to even cut the grass in the fields around the house. Nobody will come to work there for you,' he had said happily, staring at the figures on the cheque she had given him. She too was happy getting the house for almost a song.

Maya managed on her own in the huge house, cooking and cleaning, though sometimes she just let the chores pile up as she read all day under the ancient magnolia tree.

An old man would come up from the village once a week bringing her provisions and firewood and leaving hurriedly as soon as she paid him.

She was happy to live all alone and have nobody to complain about the messy clutter she surrounded herself with. Friends visiting Kasauli, a popular hill station nearby, sometimes dropped in but soon left, unable to bear the vast, gloomy house and its musty smell. 'They probably can't bear my awful cooking,' Maya thought and laughed. She was content to live a solitary life, surrounded by her books, in this broken-down house. Her only company was a fox that dropped by most evenings to hunt for pheasants and hares in the forest near her house.

~

A log of wood burnt and then hissed angrily in the fireplace as if in protest. She pushed it with the iron poker and the orange flames now flickered and rose, sending up a shower of fiery arrows, and Maya felt the soothing warmth on her face. Thunder roared and rumbled as it leapt over the mountains and the windowpanes began to rattle. Maya was not afraid of thunderstorms. In this remote mountain village, it was a part of their everyday life. She continued to read.

Then suddenly the electricity went off and the room was plunged into darkness. Only the flickering orange light of the smouldering log in the fireplace remained, bravely spreading its warmth all over the room and Maya reluctantly put her book down.

This time the touch was so gentle and light that Maya thought she had imagined it. She rubbed her neck and looked around. She was alone in this vast room, cluttered with her books and papers. Then her clothes, drying in front of the fireplace, began to tremble as if a breeze was blowing through the room. The house became eerily quiet and even the rain now fell soundlessly. Maya heard a soft whisper and strained to listen. It sounded as if someone was walking stealthily on the roof. 'It must be the fox,' thought Maya.

Then she felt fingers pressing down on the back of her neck. She could feel a hand, a cold and clammy tiny hand. It was trying to choke her. A shiver of fear ran through her and Maya suddenly felt she could not breathe. The lightning flashed again and in the fleeting silvery light, she saw the shape of a child's body to her left. It was so pale and white. Then the fingers began to move slowly, sliding all over her neck and reaching for her mouth. Maya tried to scream, but the hand now clamped itself over her mouth and she heard a soft giggle near her face.

The child, she was sure it was a child, was now caressing her face and laughing softly. Maya could only make out a faint outline of the child's face but the hands, tiny and beautiful, as if carved out of marble, were clasped firmly around her neck.

'Mama,' whispered the child and the hands began to pummel her cheeks. 'Mama,' said the child again in a louder voice and now Maya saw it was little girl. She was a little more distinct and her golden hair floated around her head like a shimmering halo. Her eyes were a faded blue. Her lips were white.

Maya tried to breathe slowly to calm herself down. 'I am not afraid. This girl is a figment of my vivid imagination. I will think of other things and she will disappear. Calm down. Think of happy things,' she repeated this over and over again to herself but the fear now rose in waves, overwhelming her. Her breathing became faster and then the clammy hands began pinching her neck and pulling her hair.

'Mama…Mama,' the child began to wail and her hands grew heavier around Maya's neck. An invisible weight now stretched itself over her back and Maya could not move. She felt the hands leave her neck and now cold arms were wrapping themselves around her, and when she tried to free herself, the arms twisted around her tightly like a snake; like a python winding itself around its prey in a fatal embrace.

Maya sat frozen with terror, her body trapped under the invisible weight. The rain lashed silently against the windowpanes and lightning streaked across the sky. The wood had burnt itself out and the room was in total darkness now except for the two white arms around her body. They seem to glow in the dark with their own eerie light. Despite her terror-stricken state, Maya suddenly thought of the fireflies that came out in the evening to dance in her garden.

'What do you want?' she heard herself say, her breathless voice shattering the darkness.

For a few moments there was silence. Maya heard her own heart thumping wildly as if she was running. She tried to take a deep breath but began to cough. Then the arms suddenly slackened their hold and the voice, sweet and lisping, said, 'Mama. Are you angry with me?'

Maya forced herself to touch the arms wrapped around her and though the cold, damp skin repulsed her, she patted it. It was like touching a dead animal.

'Who are you ? What do you want?' asked Maya, her hands trembling with fear.

The arms tightened painfully around her now once more. The child was humming to herself and then she began to whimper, 'Mama. Why are you still angry with me? I said I am sorry. Sorry… sorry…sorry.'

The arms hugged Maya and tried to rock her as if she was a child and Maya could smell a rank, rotten odour from the child's skin.

She seemed to be sobbing now and though her tears fell on Maya's neck, they disappeared at once, leaving no trace at all.

'I am not your mother. Please tell me who you are,' said Maya.

The child suddenly pushed her hands on Maya's face, forcing her down. Maya was shocked at the strength in those fragile, tiny hands. 'She is going to kill me. She will choke me to death with those tiny hands,' thought Maya wildly.

'You are so cruel to me. You don't love me. You love Rob much more and that is why you left me. You went away, Mama,' sobbed the girl, still pushing Maya down.

~

A sudden flash of lightning lit up the entire room and Maya saw the girl clearly for the first time. She was about nine or ten years old and dressed in a long, lacy dress like an English child from the last century. Her feet were bare and covered in mud and slime and her long, golden hair was matted with dead leaves. She was so ethereal and beautiful that Maya knew she was not from this world. 'I don't want to believe it but she is not a living creature,' Maya thought and felt her heart grow cold with terror.

'Tell me your name,' Maya asked, hoping the girl would respond. Somehow talking to her made Maya feel less afraid.

'You cannot even remember my name. Why are you treating me like this, Mama?' said the girl, fixing her large faded blue eyes on Maya.

'My memory is no longer very good. So please tell me your name,' said Maya, trying to speak as normally as she could though she was finding it difficult to breathe.

'Did they hurt you too when they came for me? Look, my hands are still bleeding,' said the girl, her hands touching Maya's face gently now. Maya suddenly noticed that her tiny, white hands were stained with blood.

'Who were they? Do you remember?' asked Maya

'First tell me you are not angry with me for telling them about the gold. Say you forgive me,' whispered the girl in a soft voice.

'I forgive you,' said Maya to the shimmering halo since she could not see the girl's face now. The outline of her tiny body seem to tremble and sway as if a strong wind was blowing through the house.

'The men said they would not harm anyone in the house. They just wanted the gold we had stolen from them. Their precious gold that Father had hidden in our house. "The fools will never find it. They are just savages," he had said. But the men in the village did find out about the gold and they came to the house at night, their faces covered with cloth. Do you remember now? Have you forgotten how they beat Father and Rob with sticks? You were screaming at them, begging them to let Rob go but when they caught me, you said nothing. They dragged me out into the forest and you still said nothing. Father was no longer with us. I passed away too an hour later in the forest and yet you never came looking for me. You had your precious Rob with you and that was all that mattered to you, Mama.'

'No, no…That is not true,' shouted Maya. She could hear her voice, yet it was not her voice. Someone was within her, deep within her, struggling to speak.

'Norma, please forgive me for leaving you alone. I never thought the men would take you away,' Maya said, stammering in an attempt to be coherent in this unfamiliar voice.

'You are a liar, Mama. You made a bargain with them. They told me. They did not kill me, Mama. I slipped and fell into a gorge. The forest took me. The forest protects me now but I can't stop searching for you. I see you everywhere and I come out to talk to you but you never see me. I don't exist for you. But I found you today. The waves of lightning and thunder showed me the path and helped me to find you. Stay with me now. Don't leave your little girl. Mama, don't leave me again. I will die. I will die over and over again,' cried the voice.

Maya could no longer see her and only her sobs pierced the empty darkness. The outline of her little body curved itself around Maya and now she no longer felt like a heavy oppressive weight. She was as light as air and Maya could not help caressing the cold, damp skin. It did not repulse her anymore.

A wave of pity rose in her heart for this abandoned child. How had she found her way to Maya? Had they known each other in another life? Were they linked by blood ties? Maya, all alone in this world, suddenly felt a deep love for this child; a child who lived in another world. It was a strange feeling to reach out to someone who was not there. But somehow it felt right; it felt as if it was meant to be.

~

Maya opened her eyes. Dawn was breaking over the mountain peaks and it was still raining. A cloud of mist rose up and floated into the house as if searching for someone; for something. Maya, startled, looked up, as she heard a soft footstep. There was no one. The room, untidy and familiar, stared back at her. Birds began to call outside in the garden and she heard the sound of a flute playing far away on the hillside. The rains had washed the dust off the leaves and now they glistened in the mild sunlight.

'I will always be here for you,' she heard herself say as she stumbled out of the house, her face wet with tears that vanished as soon as they touched her skin. She walked up the winding path that snaked its way around the hillside, her feet slippery on the wet, rain-soaked earth. Far away in the shadows of the forest, she caught a fleeting glimpse of a white dress and then it vanished. Maya turned back, suddenly struck by a fierce pang of longing in her heart. For the first time in her life she felt the dull ache of loneliness. She felt abandoned, just like the little girl whose touch still lingered on the back of her neck.

Then she remembered the little arms hugging her tightly and a sudden spark of joy filled her heart. She was grateful to the unseen powers for sending this child to her. She knew that they would meet again and again, till Maya passed into her shadowy world one day. The thought filled her with happiness and she began to walk quickly all the way down to her storm-ravaged house to wait for the little girl—her invisible child.

17

A Revenge in Thread

When Ashima saw the envelope, she burst into tears. There was no need for grief because it did not contain a card announcing someone's funeral. It was an invitation to her sister's daughter's wedding. She had not seen her sister for almost fifteen years. This daughter must be nineteen years old now; nineteen years and three months exactly. Her name when she was born was Parul but now they called her Mondira.

Ashima wiped the tears from the wedding card, which was red with a huge gold and pink lotus in the centre. It was wrapped in gold tissue paper and tied with red and green silken thread. It looked expensive and gaudy. She would have never chosen a flashy card like this. She would have chosen a simple design, maybe a tiny garland of red flowers on pale cream paper.

But she was not the mother—not anymore. She had given her daughter away. No. They had forced her to give away her baby girl nineteen years and three months ago.

Ashima tried hard not to think about her lost child. She had her sons to take care of, her lazy good-for-nothing husband to worry about and the household to manage. But sometimes at night, when the moon shone through the window, covering her bed in a glinting light and she could not sleep, the terrible day came back to her.

She watched herself crying silently; she counted the minutes, waiting for the pain to end. Then the moon vanished behind the clouds, darkness fell around her and all was calm. As she listened to her husband's gentle snores, her face wet with tears, she tried once again to erase those painful memories about her lost child; she tried and failed again.

~

It was dawn when Parul finally came out of her womb, screaming like a fishwife, an ugly bundle of blood and mucus.

'Oh! We see bad, bad temper here,' said the midwife, laughing as she held the baby upside down as if it was a freshly killed chicken. 'I better give her a little slap, just to remind her she is a woman and not a prince who can show his temper to the world.' Ashima saw her slap the baby hard on her bottom a few times. She remembered before she drifted off to sleep again that her brave little girl had screamed even louder.

Had they made her docile now with regular beatings? Or had they let her grow up spoilt and wilful? She was very pretty, people said. She was the only child of rich parents and she would get a good husband, people said.

Many years ago Ashima had waited outside her school, hoping to catch a glimpse of her but when the bell rang and all the girls rushed out, she did not know what to do. How would she recognize her daughter who she had not seen for ten years ? She watched, panic-stricken, as all the girls ran past her, each one looking like her own flesh and blood.

'Let her go, Ashima. Give her to your sister. She will grow up in a wealthy home. You already have three boys. Think of their future. If you please rich relatives, it always helps everyone in the family. We will never get a chance like this. This is our moment to trap them forever in our debt. Give her away. She is only a girl. They are a burden on the family,' her mother said, stroking her palm, cajoling her.

Her father, usually quiet and mild-mannered, became surprisingly agitated when they came to take Parul away.

'Ma moni…are you sure? I do not want you to have any regrets later. You can refuse if you do not want to give your baby girl away,' he said, but he took care to whisper so that her mother could not hear. But her mother's sharp ears caught every word.

'No, she cannot refuse now. She promised her sister and I have told Rani the baby is hers. It was all decided before she was born, remember? If Ashima had a girl this time, we would give it to her. Be happy she is not asking for one of your sons,' her mother said, giving her husband a sharp look, surprised and annoyed by his bold behaviour. In thirty years of their peaceful wedded life he had never once contradicted her. 'So the old man still has a bit of fire left in him. I must douse it at once,' she thought and swiftly turned around. Narrowing her eyes into strips of black, she aimed them like darts towards her husband. She twisted her mouth into a jagged curve—a formidable combination of a grimace and a smile. It never failed to work. Her husband looked down at his feet and began mumbling nervously. She watched him for a moment, making sure he was his old, obedient self and then said loudly, 'So all is decided and we are all happy now.' She smiled at them, picked up the baby and walked out of the room. The door slammed shut.

~

The door always slammed shut when her mother finished talking. Even now when she was a senile old woman muttering incoherently all day to her long dead husband, screaming at people only she could see, Ashima still feared her mother's voice. She still feared to be reprimanded by her.

They gave her baby away nineteen years and three months ago and she had never stopped regretting it every day of her life. She tried very hard not to think about her loss, pretending nothing had happened, but the pain clung to her, hiding in the corners of her mind. At night suddenly two small hands would grab her neck and two tiny eyes would gleam in the darkness. Sometimes when she was alone in the house, she heard a baby wailing but she could never find it.

'You are mad. Just forget her now. She would have been just an extra mouth to feed,' her husband said. 'Look at our healthy, handsome boys. How well they are growing now that we can give them better food to eat.' Her daughter was a weed they uprooted and threw out so that their sons could have more sunlight to grow taller, healthier and stronger.

She wished she could see her just once so that she could remember her face for the rest of her life, but her mother did not want her to visit her sister or see her daughter. 'People might find out and then they will call your poor sister barren,' she said. At first her sister Rani wrote her letters telling her how Parul, now renamed Mondira, was growing up, sharing small things about her, like her first word—'bandhu'; her favourite food—'bananas', but then after a few years the letters stopped. Ashima was not invited ever to visit. The door was slammed shut once more. Her sons were never told they had a sister. Her husband forgot he had once had a daughter.

Now nineteen years and three months later, Ashima held her daughter's wedding invitation in her hand. She was surprised they had invited her. Maybe now there was no longer any danger of her snatching her child back or people talking. Ashima carefully put the wedding card in her sewing basket. Then she took out a deep red thread and began sewing flowers on the soft cloth. She embroidered at night when the moonlight did not let her sleep. She lit a lamp and sat near the window, making tiny stitches in the cloth, thinking about her child. Sometimes her husband woke up and muttered angrily, but she ignored him and he went back to sleep.

He had never cared for their baby girl. 'Let her go. We will save the dowry money. The boys can have a bit more,' he had said. 'Your sister's husband is so rich, if we please him, he might find jobs for our sons when they grow up,' he added, sounding just like her mother. She sometimes thought they had plotted this together. Rani, the rich daughter, should be kept happy and what did poor, insignificant Ashima's sorrow matter? Her husband often sat up at night planning what they would do with all the money her baby daughter would bring. A girl who brought in money was a rare thing; a rare, precious thing which could be bartered only once in a lifetime.

Her sister's husband had been generous with money and gifts. He had paid for the boys' education in a good school, for Ashima's operation, for the roof of their house to be repaired, and for her husband's new dentures. Her little baby girl had made life easier for everyone but Rani's wealth could not do anything to take away the pain, which dug its claws deep into her heart at night.

~

She had finished embroidering sixteen flowers and still had three more to do. One flower for each year she had not seen her and three tiny leaves for the months. A wedding gift for her daughter who would never know it was from her mother. What would she say when she saw her daughter for the first time? Would her face be like hers, a reflection of her own features or would she be different? She would have to be very calm and careful when they met for the first time. Her mother and her sister would be watching her.

As her fingers flew over the soft cloth, Ashima suddenly began to embroider a face. It was a small, ugly face with huge eyes and a bald head. A baby's face. Then a screaming mouth emerged. She tried to turn it into a flower, quickly putting in a plain chain stitch, but the needle seemed to move on its own. Ashima watched her fingers fly, her heart beating rapidly as the images began to form on the cloth. She made a line, a curve, but it made itself into a strange shape. Eyes, mouths and heads appeared as if by magic. She tried to make a leaf but then after a few stitches the needle ran away from her. She had never worked so fast. The cloth was covered within minutes. There was no empty place left anymore. Flowers, half-opened buds, birds and butterflies danced about and hidden beneath them were the faces; her father looking at her helplessly, her husband's gaping, greedy mouth, her mother's victorious smile, entwined with her sister's proud, arrogant eyes. In one little corner, surrounded by trees and flowering creepers, stood an empty cot and above it loomed her own face staring out blankly.

The faces wove themselves in and out of the flowers and birds. Now a baby emerged out of nowhere—her baby, and crawled all over the soft cotton cloth, then as she stitched, the baby grew into a girl. She ran and skipped through the garden as her fingers stitched faster and faster. The needle pricked her thumb and the blood seeped into the cloth, merging into the red and orange flowers.

Her head was spinning, her fingers were stiff with pain and she could no longer see clearly. Then the needle fell from her fingers and was lost in the darkness. The moonlight shone on the cloth which was now covered with hundreds of intricate stitches, each one a fragment of her life.

~

Ashima sat with her head bowed for a long time and when she lifted her head, it was dawn. Her mother was quiet for once and the house was still. Her sons were away in the city. They worked for her sister's husband. Her whole family were slaves to her sister who never let them forget it. Her mother had said that it was good to have rich people in your debt but she was wrong.

'You were wrong, Ma, for once in your life you made a mistake,' she shouted to the empty walls.

'I will be forever in her debt. I am forever chained to her because she has my child and my heart in the palm of her hand.'

Dawn was breaking when Ashima picked up the cloth. She found the needle was still embedded in it. There was a small empty place left and she wrote her name, but quickly hid it under a curling leaf. She cut the thread off and then laid it aside. Her sister would open it and the faces would stare back at her and she would know, but only she would know, what the kantha said. Her daughter would only see the beautiful flowers, the dancing birds and the floating leaves, but her sister would see the hidden faces. She would feel Ashima's sorrow, her pain, each time she saw the kantha and that would be her revenge. A petty revenge but that was all she could do. Ashima gently wrapped the kantha in a red silk bag and went out of the room as the door slammed shut.

18

Toofan

It was beginning to get dark and the gate light had already been switched on. It cast a dim circle of dusty yellow light on the ground. The boy had still not returned. 'He has gone. I knew he would,' Meena thought mechanically, again and again as she leaned out of the window. The words hammered inside her head in a dull monotone and, though she tried to turn deaf, as she often did, she had to listen to them.

The window was wide open, but she took care not to lean too far out because she knew her mother was watching her. 'Why are you hanging out of the window? He will not come back. Stop behaving like an idiot,' she said in a soft whisper. Her mother had talked in this hushed, feeble voice for as long as Meena could remember. Her childhood memories were sharply punctuated by these breathless words, always cruel, always complaining, except when a third person was present. Then her mother's voice changed. It was still a whisper but it became soft and helpless as she praised Meena. 'This girl will not think of herself at all. Day and night she looks after me, does not leave me even for a minute. I tell her, Beta, what will you do when I am gone?' A brave smile and a graceful flutter of hands accompanied this voice and the listener never failed to respond with an indulgent smile.

Meena hated this gentle husky tone and automatically shut her ears when her mother talked like this. She did not mind the cruel, hurtful, comments. She had got used to the nagging that went on as persistently as water dripping from a leaking tap, but this sweet voice, which she called her mother's drawing room voice, told her each time how much her mother disliked her.

Meena moved away from the window to restrain herself from looking at the gate again. But she listened carefully for footsteps and watched Sheru to see if his ears were twitching. The dog always knew when Toofan was at the gate and would start growling softly. He had never got used to the boy and, though he never attacked him, he would snarl whenever he saw him. 'Maybe he teases him,' her mother said but Meena had never seen Toofan ever go near the dog.

Toofan was not his real name. 'I do not know what name my mother gave me. She died when I was born and my father could not remember. They called me Chotu at home but I like Toofan. After all, I will not stay Chotu all my life, will I?' he asked her, looking up at her and laughing, as if they were old friends. Her mother was against keeping him in their house. 'He might have some disease. They are all illegitimate and they all have VD, you know,' she said, rolling her eyes sideways as she did when she wanted to shock someone. Meena did not know what VD was, except that it was something secret, to do with sex and that it only happened to poor people. She had seen the letters painted on walls near slum colonies and was shocked that her mother, who had not stepped out of the house except to go to the club to play cards once a week and to the hairdresser's to get her hair dyed once a month, knew these shameful words. Toofan looked so untouched by anything despite his dirty clothes that Meena told him he could stay, as long as he slept in the garage. But she looked up VD in the medical encyclopaedia that night and though she was still not sure what exactly it was, she blushed as she read the brief clinical description. She gave the boy a bottle of Dettol next day and told him to bathe in it. 'All over, you must wash all over,' she said, almost choking over the words with embarrassment. For a few days he obeyed her and the house smelt like a hospital ward as he walked about, leaving a trail of disinfectant. Then he stopped bathing in Dettol. 'It makes my skin itch,' he said and scratched his thin arm, covered with mosquito bites and prickly heat, to demonstrate a streak of red lines to her. Meena did not insist anymore and now the house reeked of the flowery hair oil that he used to plaster down his sun-bleached hair.

Toofan had run away from home at the age of nine or ten, he was not sure. The story of his life changed every day and he hated being reminded of anything he had said earlier. 'I do not remember,' he would say and then stare at her with a sullen look. Meena, who in her forty-six years had never spoken an untruth, was intimidated by this defiant, boastful lying. She kept quiet and did not question him anymore when he talked, though at first, the lies made her uneasy and confused. Gradually, she got used to his wild talk and did not care whether he was telling the truth or not. Soon she began to believe every word. After Toofan had run away from home, he had lived at the railway station for two years, working as a coolie and sometimes begging on the trains or cleaning cars in parking lots. He had worked as a labourer on a bridge-building site, joined a circus for a short time and had even been a holy man's assistant for a few days and walked all the way to Badrinath with him. Every month he went with his friends to Bombay though they had never bought a train ticket. 'We pretend to be deaf and dumb when the ticket checker comes.' It seemed to Meena that he had done more in his short life than was possible in a lifetime, at least judging from her own unmarked, placid forty-six years. 'Most of it is lies. These people cannot open their mouths without lying. It is in their blood, like thieving and producing endless babies,' her mother reminded her each time, like a recorded message when Toofan began telling them some amazing story, full of horror, bravado and unbelievable violence. But Meena, with her well-trained ears, glimpsed the truth in the boy's stories just as clearly as she picked out each lying syllable in her mother's drawing room voice and as she listened to the boy, his life, so strange and bewildering, gradually became more real to her than her own.

Meena had always lived in this town and in this house. She still slept on the bed on which she had been born, and her toys, unbroken and almost new after so many years, still lined the shelves. There was a greyish black patch on the wall of her bedroom where she had splashed ink one day in a rare fit of anger. Though the wall had been painted many times since, the dark stain always managed to seep out. The first half of her life was buried under the claustrophobic care of her parents and her childhood was spent learning how to ignore their horror when they looked at her deformed body. The later years passed by on their own without her, as she changed roles with her ageing parents. The clubfoot, which had brought so much sorrow to her parents and set her apart from the rest of the world, changed too, without her knowing. Though she still walked with a limp, it had now become a clumsy but natural movement of her body as it grew heavy and awkward with middle age. Now only she and her mother remained in the large, musty house, each accusing the other of wrongs they had both long forgotten. They were content until the boy arrived.

But now he was not going to come back, they could go back to their lives. Meena took out a book and began to read. The words were like small black spots. Her mother burped and then gave a satisfied sigh. 'We will go to the doctor tomorrow,' she said, as if promising Meena a treat. Meena had enjoyed these monthly trips to the clinic before Toofan came. She used to dress up for the occasion. Her mother did too. It gave them a chance to wear their best saris and spray on perfume. Meena liked going to the clinic better than going to the club where everyone was older, more malicious and more sick than her mother. They took turns to talk about their illnesses and only looked at her once during the evening to ask about her foot. They made her lift her sari so that they could sigh over it though she herself had forgotten how ugly it was. She would never go there again. Journeys were only real if Toofan had talked about them.

Meena had only been out of this town twice in forty-six years. Once to Haridwar, when they had taken her father's ashes and then for a family wedding to Calcutta with her mother. Both the trips had been equally unhappy, the wedding with its gaiety which excluded her, even more than the funeral journey, where her mother for once had been too shocked and grief-stricken to attack her. Meena could tell Toofan the story of her life in five or maybe six (if she added her various childhood illnesses) sentences, but Toofan did not want to know. Like all children he assumed that the only world that existed was the one in which he lived. He talked about himself and he assumed that Meena wanted to listen to him just as much as he did. And he was right. She loved the way his eyes grew big with surprise as he amazed and impressed himself with his own stories. Sometimes they became so dramatic and unreal that even Meena could not believe them, however much she wanted to. Her mother liked listening to him too, but she never did it openly. She pretended to be asleep when Toofan talked, but Meena often noticed that her eyelids would flicker. Once she suddenly hissed in a broken whisper, 'You liar, that is what happened in *Coolie*. I have just seen that film on TV.' Toofan was startled by this sudden interruption and looked sheepish for a moment or two, but he quickly recovered to say, 'I am also a coolie, Mataji.' Meena, who hardly ever saw any films did not know what they were talking about. But her mother was pleased to have caught the boy out and went to sleep that afternoon with a quiet smile on her face.

And now he was not going to come back. Each time he left them, Meena feared that he would never return. And when he did come back she was still anxious and waited for him to leave again. She often wished she had never allowed him to come into the house. She should have let him remain outside like the stray cat that she fed sometimes. Then she would not have expected anything from him. Now he neither belonged to her nor was he one of the many faceless children on the street, who did not exist for her except when she felt sorry for them.

It was quite dark now and Meena could not see the road beyond the gate anymore. 'He will not come back. These boys are like stray dogs, they can never stay in one place,' she heard her mother say but she did not turn around. 'Will you give me my dinner now or do I have to starve till the wretch comes home? Are you planning to hang out of the window like an idiot all night so that the neighbours can laugh at us?' her mother hissed. 'Shut that window now.' Meena turned away from the window and went to the kitchen. The dog followed her. She told the maid to heat up the food and she slowly began counting out the forks and spoons as she did when Toofan had been here. She was trying to teach the boy to count but she was not sure whether he was a fast learner or that he already knew and was trying to fool her. At first he had seemed so helpless but gradually, Meena began to see flashes of a sly cleverness in his eyes. 'He would need every bit of craftiness in his small body to survive the way he has done,' Meena told herself, but she liked to recall his innocent face, the one he had on the first day she had seen him. 'Can I polish your car, memsahib?' he had said and she had allowed him because he had not called her Mataji as the other urchins did. She gave him five rupees and some fruits that she had just bought. 'I will come to your house and clean the car,' he announced, and turned up that same evening.

'How did you find my house?' Meena asked him, strangely pleased. 'I followed you. I ran behind your car. It is not far from the market.' At first he used to clean the car and go away, but after Meena began leaving bits of leftover food for him, he began to hang around the house.

Once she found him sleeping in the garage, covered with an old towel which had once belonged to the dog. She gave him an old blanket the next day. 'Just make sure you don't touch him. They have skin diseases, these people,' her mother said, but she did not mind when he came into the kitchen to wash the dishes when the maid did not turn up one day. Toofan gradually started coming into the house, creeping in step by step, and now he lived with them all the time, doing odd jobs around the house.

Today she had given him a hundred rupees to buy medicines for her mother. She wanted to test his honesty but at the same time, in a strange way, she wanted him to run away with the money. Then she could dismiss him as a thief and forget about him. It would be a relief and she could go back to selling cards for UNICEF, to ease her conscience, much easier than this cat and mouse game with this boy.

'They are all thieves and pickpockets. You think by bathing him in Dettol and giving him good food you will change him? What do you think he is, a dog? You have been fooled. He has taken the money and gone back to the station to gamble it away.' Her mother as usual had read her thoughts, picked them clean of any weak, wavering kindness and spat the words back at her. Meena watched her as she chewed her food slowly, her eyes narrow and gleaming with satisfaction. 'Are you sure you washed my dentures this morning? They feel dirty.' Meena ate silently. She had taught herself to shut out the voice many years ago and now even when she wanted to listen her ears clamped themselves shut.

It was well after midnight when Toofan came back. She was awake, reading, and suddenly the dog began to growl. Meena forced herself to remain sitting and slowly reached out to trace a word with her fingertip. She strained her ears to listen for any footsteps and when Sheru began to bark, she sat back in her chair with relief. Her mother complained about the noise next morning but only when she saw him after breakfast. 'Whole night I was awake because of this boy. I had to take two Calmpose tablets yet I could not shut my eyes. I told you the wretch would be back. Where will he go? All this pampering, free food where will he get? Only in the dharamshala my daughter is running!' her mother said, picking at her teeth with tiny, angry stabs.

Toofan did not say why he was so late and Meena did not want to ask him. He had a deep cut above his eye but when Meena wanted to wash it with Dettol, he would not allow her to do so. 'You like this Dettol so much. You even smell like it,' he said, laughing and pinching his nose in mock disgust. Meena did not say anything but she went and washed her hands with her mother's Camay soap which she only used when she went to the club. But when Meena smelt her hands, a faint odour of disinfectant still remained.

Toofan did not go out at all for many days. He sat with the chowkidar at the gate in the evenings and talked in a low voice. Sometimes he looked up at the house and laughed in a shrill screaming, cackle which made Sheru bark. Meena knew that he would soon get bored and leave again. She did not know how to amuse a child. What made them happy, she wondered all day. She tried but could not remember what had made her happy when she was a child. The next day she bought him some books and began teaching him the alphabet. 'Just teach me some English words. What good will all this book learning do,' he said each time they sat down to study.

One day when he bent down to read, Meena noticed that he had a deep scar on his back. 'How did that happen?' she asked. 'A mad woman stabbed me once. I have many scars, you want to see?' Before Meena could reply, Toofan took off his shirt and proudly displayed a network of faint brown marks on his chest. 'I got this when I hid from the police. You remember that day when I came back so late? There was a police raid at the station. Some boys were caught, but I escaped. They can never catch me. Each time they come I hide under a car.' Toofan jumped up and then lay down flat on the floor. He rolled himself up in a ball like a baby monkey. 'See, this is how I hide under a car. Even when the policeman bends down he can't see me.'

'What happened to the money I gave you that day?' Meena asked, not looking up from the books.

'I-I lost it,' Toofan replied and began reading aloud the words she had taught him.

The next day he went away. Meena came back from the library where she worked and before she entered the house, she somehow knew he had gone.

'Good riddance,' her mother whispered but when they went out to the club, she suddenly shouted, 'There he is. Catch him!' but it was another boy, just as dirty and ragged, not Toofan. A week went by and Toofan was still not back. Meena stopped watching the gate and now sat with her back to the window. But her mother took over the watch and though she cursed the boy in a low whisper, she placed her chair close to the window and often called out to the chowkidar. 'Has he come, the beggar? I think he will come back today.' Now Meena wanted her mother to move away from the window. She feared that her eagerness would bring bad luck and the boy would never return. Her mother had never got what she wanted. Did she not always complain without fail every day? 'God has never given me a single good thing.' Why should He change his mind now about her mother. Day after day they sat, one with her back to the window and the other staring out, experiencing a companionship they had never felt before. Meena, to distract her mother, began to talk to her. The old lady, willing to be distracted, listened. Both waited for the boy.

Months went by and the waiting gradually lost its anxiety and became a habit. They had almost forgotten his face when one night Toofan came back. Meena had just shut the window and was about to turn off the light. Then suddenly she held her breath. Someone was running in the street. A boy…maybe…no it could not be. Then she heard the gate creak. Meena still did not go to the window. And then Sheru growled. 'Meena, Meena. Go and see…' her mother called out from the bed. 'Please, God, please let her not say anything more. Please do not listen to her.' Meena stood exactly where she was, as if afraid that any movement she made would stop the footsteps that were coming closer. The garage door opened and then Meena knew it was Toofan. She called out through the window, loudly, with slight irritation, now no longer afraid that it would not be him.

They waited for him to say something but he just stared blankly at the window. His clothes were torn and his knees had blood on them. He stood in an awkward way with his back bent and Meena noticed for the first time, how thin his legs were. 'Don't stand there like an idiot. Come inside,' her mother called out to him in a laughing soft voice Meena had not heard before. Her old face was full of eager anticipation for some bad news. Suddenly, Meena wanted to take the boy away from her mother. But Toofan came and sat by her bed. He curled up and began shivering. 'What is wrong with you? Have you got malaria or what? Don't sit so close to me. Meena, take him to the servant's quarter. Make him bathe first.' But then her curiosity overcame her fear of infection and she hissed, 'Where were you all these days, you dirty beggar? Must have been in jail.'

Toofan looked at her, his eyes blind with fear. 'They told you? They came here too?' Meena caught hold of his hand and dragged him up. 'You first eat something. Come.' They went to the kitchen. Toofan slumped on the floor and began shivering again. 'The boys who could not hide were caught and put into the van and taken to the children's jail. Tana, Ramu, Chuttan. Now they will never come out. They will become old and die. They beat us every day. Chuttan's hand is broken. I escaped…last night, a tree fell on the wall. I ran here. They won't come here, will they? You won't tell them?' Meena wanted to reassure him and began to say the soothing words, but she did not speak. His fear would keep him with her forever. It would chain him to her and not allow him to ever leave her. She would look after him, maybe even send him to school, give him money to buy whatever he wanted, give him all the freedom he asked for and he would always come back. Every day, they would talk about the truth that awaited him outside the safe circle of her shelter. The shadow of the children's home would always hover over him, the filth of his life, the abuse, the beatings would remain just a step away. And every day she would make his life happier, soothe away his fears but take care never to heal the scars. Toofan would never go away now, and even if he did, she knew he would always come back because he had nowhere to go. 'Let me wash the blood off from your legs. I won't put Dettol. Then you eat your food and go to sleep. Tomorrow you can tell me everything that happened,' Meena said gently in a whisper and was surprised to hear herself speaking in her mother's drawing room voice. He gave her a surprised look and then they both burst out laughing, for no reason.

19

Radha and N Dead

N Dead wraps her clammy hands around my neck and whispers. 'You know you had a twin brother.'

I am startled by her words and turn my head quickly towards her voice. 'What are you saying? Where is he? Are you lying to me again?'

'If you don't believe what I say then I won't talk to you,' she says angrily. I feel her presence ebbing away from me like a plume of smoke I had seen many years ago when I could see. My heart fills with fear.

'No. No. I am sorry. Don't go. Please don't go. I believe you. Where is this brother of mine. Have you seen him?' I ask.

'I saw him when he was born,' says N Dead.

'Why did they never tell me about him?' I ask. I feel my heart churning with a strange sorrow. Had I seen him when my eyes could see? I try very hard to think back to my early childhood but I see nothing except for a few trembling shapes. I am not sure if they are N Dead's fellow ghosts hovering on the horizon of my mind or real people I had glimpsed when my eyes were not blind. (A word of explanation: N Dead is the ghost of my grandmother, Nilanjana Devi, who along with several other ghosts of my ancestors, has taken up residence in our house in Shimla. N Dead had attached herself to me and would regale me with stories of relatives, alive or dead, when the mood took her.)

'What was the point of telling you? They did not want to add to your anxiety. You were such a difficult child as it is. Constantly having nightmares, wetting your bed and screaming hysterically all night,' said N Dead.

'Did my brother look like me?' I ask.

'No. He was very handsome. He was much fairer than you and had golden hair. He looked like a plump English baby when he was born. The English matron in the Shimla hospital was surprised that he was an Indian baby. Your grandfather took him home right away though the matron said the mother and baby should stay a few days longer in the hospital. He was worried that the matron would steal him.'

'How did he just vanish?'

'Maybe he died. I think someone stole him. Many boys were abducted from the Shimla Mall that summer. They said some sadhu who had come to give a discourse in Shimla from Benaras had stolen half a dozen small boys and taken them back to his ashram. This man who died outside your door was also from Benaras. God always sends people to repent their sins.' (Another word of explanation: a visitor, a man whom I had never seen before, had come to our house earlier, and was found dead at the bottom of the stairs the next morning.)

'Could he have seen my brother in Benaras? Maybe he came to tell my father about him?' I ask. N Dead does not reply.

'You know, I saw this man in my dreams once,' I say hesitantly. 'I was standing on top of the stairs and I saw him lying on the ground. I could see him clearly. There was blood around his head.'

'Don't talk to me about your silly dreams. I live in a dream all the time and I hate listening to anyone else's dreams,' says N Dead, and I can feel her moving away from me.

'Don't go. Tell me about my twin brother. Take me to Benaras. Please, don't go,' I beg her. I put my hand out to touch her.

N Dead stretches herself out on my shoulders.

'My father was the chief priest at the Kashi Vishwanath temple. People touched his feet when he walked down the lanes of Benaras and my mother had to walk ten steps behind him. Your grandfather saw me one morning when I was standing on the terrace of the temple drying my hair. Your grandfather said he wanted to marry me as soon as I turned my face to look at him standing on the street below but I don't remember all this at all,' said N Dead.

'Have you never gone back to revisit such an important moment in your life?' I ask. I am surprised N Dead is talking so much about herself today. I want her to tell me about my lost brother but I do not want to disturb her chain of memories. She might get annoyed and leave. I don't want her to leave. I want someone to be with me.

~

The new girl Bala has gone somewhere. I heard her footsteps leaving the room. I must tell her to ask my permission before going anywhere. She has so much to learn but it will be interesting to teach a new person. I have never done it before. It is good to have someone at your constant beck and call, like an obedient slave, just like I am a slave for N Dead.

N Dead comes closer. I feel her cool, musty breath on my face. 'I don't like to go into my life that has swept past me into the beyond. Waste of time. Why should I live through all that again. I take you to your parents' past lives because you are so full of curiosity, and besides you have no life of your own. I help you to live through their lives. What else do you have, you poor blind girl. Do you think I like going into my own life? I hate looking into my past. Your grandfather might have fallen in love with me when he saw me for the first time but I wanted to marry someone else. My father would have never have allowed it since he was from another caste, so I accepted your grandfather. What other choice did I have? Your sister married someone she liked, someone your parents had not chosen for her. But in my time we had to bow our heads and accept whatever was given to us. Good or bad, our lives were chosen for us by our fathers and if they turned out happy it was our good luck, but if we were beaten, starved, and burnt to death, it was our bad luck. Whatever it was, we were to blame. Finally, in death I am free to choose and I choose not to go into my past life. Now let me tell you about the day your father tried to drive a motor car,' says N Dead. I agree readily.

'Was my twin brother there?' I ask, trying to bring her mind back to my lost brother, my lost twin with whom I had shared my mother's womb for nine months. The same blood, the same skin must have joined us. Ten fingers for him and ten for me, four ears, ten toes, four eyes but I got the two blind ones. He could see with his two eyes but then why did he get lost? Where is he?

'Yes, your brother was there sitting in the pram with you. I saw you both near the verandah. One ugly dark child and one fair handsome one. We heard the noise of the car before we saw it. It came at top speed through the gates. There were two stone lions on the gatepost and one of them fell off. Your father saw it falling and tried to avoid it. He drove right into the gate, the car jumped up a few feet and landed on the lawn. The engine began smoking and we all rushed out and pulled your father out. The driver who was teaching him to drive had fainted in the back seat. It took a long time to get him out since he was a huge, hefty man from the village—a former truck driver. Both, your father and he, never drove again. But how your father loved telling this story to everyone in Asansol. For days people came to see the car, surprisingly undamaged, perched on the lawn by the lily pond. Your mother had to serve tea and snacks to so many people that she just ordered the local bakery to send boxes full of cakes and biscuits every morning.'

~

I lie in bed and think about my twin brother. Where could he have gone? Why can't N Dead find him? I ask her and she says, 'I try but I also have limits, you know. I cannot see everything. I cannot show you everything.' She is in a bad mood now. We sit quietly and listen to the noise going on downstairs. We are not going anywhere today since another feast is about to begin.

My mother comes into my room, complaining about the cost. 'Your father wants a puja done for the dead man from Benaras too. The priest insists on it since our house is polluted by this sudden death and must be cleansed. Everything will cost double now. We have to donate two sets of clothes, brass utensils, beddings and umbrellas now to the priest. I could have bought a new diamond necklace with the money your father is wasting on this double feast. The man was not even a relative of ours. Choto Dadu insists we are related but I don't remember his face. The police are now sure he was pushed down the stairs and are hunting for his murderer. How could this have happened in the house? I think they are all making a big mistake,' she says and asks me to rub balm on her forehead. I have very soft hands, you know, and everyone asks me to rub balm on their foreheads. I don't mind doing it since I like to be of some use. I sit with my mother's head in my lap and I know from her breathing that she has gone to sleep.

Outside my window, I can hear the wind rustle through the pine trees. I can hear each tree sigh; each tree has a separate sound. The trees too have moods. I can hear them hiss angrily and then murmur gently to each other. Sometimes I lie awake at night and listen to them crying softly. What sorrow could a tree have? Whose loss do they bear? Who do they mourn?

After my mother wakes up and goes away, the room is quiet. I know I am alone since I cannot hear anything moving at all in the room, not even N Dead. I reach my arms out into the velvety darkness and feel nothing. My ears strain to pick up any vibrations but there is just empty silence all around me. Suddenly I am afraid. What if someone is standing very still and watching me? What if they are very close but I cannot feel their presence. My heart begins to race and I clutch at the sheet. 'Who is there?' I call out and the sound of my voice cuts the empty space and falls back on me. I turn my head towards the window, towards the lighter shade of black, where I know there must be some light since it is not yet evening, and wait. I can hear only my heartbeat and nothing else at all. Then the raven begins to call and suddenly a cold hand touches my face. I smile. I know I am still alive and my beloved ghost is by my side.

~

The next day the boy who works in the garden comes to the window and tells me that the police suspect a moneylender from his village had followed the dead man here. 'They are checking for footprints in the garden,' says the boy, his voice quivering with excitement. This man apparently had borrowed a huge amount of money from the moneylender in his village and refused to pay him back. 'He could have been killed by one of the moneylender's goondas.'

'But how did they get into our house? Did no one see them?' I ask, and the boy says he does not know. I know he is staring at me. I know he is shrugging his shoulders. 'We never saw anything, Didi.'

Now his voice sounds guilty as if he was responsible for letting this killer into the house. Later, as evening falls outside my window and flowers release their scent as the light begins to fade, my mother comes and sits on my bed and talks to me while N Dead repeats the funeral feast menu over and over again. Their voices, sweet and shrill, merge in my head like a gurgling stream and I try to concentrate to understand both.

N Dead wins because her voice echoes right inside my head.

'Big galda prawns cooked with mustard. Fried eggplant, cauliflower, mung dal, fish curry with fresh coconut milk, and many other dishes. I wish I was alive and could eat. Death has taken away my need for food but left the taste buds intact. So cruel. I sit here helpless, drooling like a hungry dog,' she complains, climbing over our heads, clinging to my neck like a damp cloth. Stuck between my mother's whining voice and N Dead's complaining one, my head begins to ache. I call Bala. She comes running to me and sits down near the bed. 'Press my feet, girl,' says my mother before I can say anything.

'After that you go and get some food for us. Go to the kitchen and tell them to send up three thalis of fish and rice,' I say.

'Three plates for whom?' my mother asks, her bangles jangling. I know she is irritated with me. I don't care. I want to send food for Bala's mother. I want to soften her, before I go out to meet this clever witch.

~

I forgot to tell you that I was not born blind. I remember seeing quite clearly till I was eight or nine years old and then my world slowly started getting blurred. But I remember the vivid colours of flowers, birds and trees. The Black Drongo, the Purple Sunbird, and the Cinnamon Sparrows. I can see them in my head when I hear their calls. When I inhale the scent of the roses growing in our garden, I know at once what colour they are. Clever, aren't I? I know what a deodar tree looks like and on the rare occasions I go out holding either Saralama's or my mother's hand, I always make them take me very close to the tree so that I can touch its rough bark, touch its sharp needle-like leaves with my fingertips till it hurts. I know what my mother's face looks like and what expression my father wears when he is talking to me but these precious memories are fading each day. I cling to these images and am afraid they will be erased totally unless I see them in my mind's eye over and over again. I have already forgotten the faces of other people I had seen in my childhood.

I know my room well. I recall every piece of furniture. I touch them every day to remind myself of their shape. I feel safe only after I touch everything in my room three times. No one ever dares to move anything in my room. But if I go anywhere new, which is very rare, then I have no idea what there is around me. My knees begin to tremble. I often stumble and I put my hands out just like a blind person. I can feel the glances of pity swirl around me. When I meet new people, I don't know what they look like. I amuse myself by thinking up their features, painting them in new colours and giving them odd shapes, but I hold my parents' faces in a secret, safe place in my head. I am so afraid they are going to disappear soon. I know one day I will wake up and no longer remember their faces.

~

The funeral feasts are finally over and I can hear the kites screeching outside my window. They must be fighting over the leftover scraps of food the servants have thrown into the backyard. A fierce dog fight breaks out under my window and then is settled quickly. They obviously don't want to waste time bickering with each other when food is to be grabbed. Saralama says a police inspector came for the dead man's feast and sat by my father's side, whispering to him all the time. He even wrote down something in his notebook.

'Uncouth man. No respect for the dead. He will be punished by the gods, you mark my words,' N Dead giggles and pokes her finger into Saralama's eyes.

Saralama feels her invisible touch like a bit of grit in her eyes and rubs them, muttering angrily to herself.

Today N Dead is in a very happy mood for some reason and keeps stroking my arm, singing me a gentle lullaby. 'Oh! my beloved who disturbs my sleep, let me sing you a song. To keep you awake, to make you remember my sadness.' It is a song by Tagore which my father hums too very often when he is shaving. N Dead has a soft, sweet voice when she sings, unlike the harsh tones she uses when she talks to me in my head. I think she can go into other people's souls and steal whatever she wants; their sweet voices, their soft hands or their fierce tempers. Today she has taken someone's meek nature, I can see. I am not sure she will stay long in this kind soul and I wonder whether I should get her to talk about the murder outside my door or about my twin brother.

Quick. I must decide quickly before she comes out of this mood and becomes her usual bossy self. But I cannot think of anything. My mind often goes blank like my eyes. I think all this travelling with N Dead into the past has exhausted me and I must rest for a while in my real life. I listen hard to discern any sounds in the room but there is no one about this morning. I can hear footsteps far away in the kitchen. If I concentrate very hard, I can even hear people talking on the road outside. I wish they had not given me a room on the first floor. I find it difficult to go down the stairs though I sometimes force myself to do so. Just to shock everyone. I suddenly appear in their midst to remind them I am still here—the forgotten blind girl. I love wallowing in self-pity sometimes. It is a comfortable feeling like eating something sweet and fried.

Actually, I am quite happy living in my dark, grey cocoon. I feel so safe, like a baby in its mother's womb. I have N Dead, my beloved ghost, by my side and I can see better than most people, through her long-dead eyes. I see everything she can see and even beyond. The only thing I hate is that I have to depend on her moods to make me feel alive. I suppose you cannot have everything in this world.

'Did I have a twin brother?' I ask my mother the next time she comes into my room

'No. Who told you such a lie?' she says, turning her head towards me so swiftly that I can hear her neck protest with a cricking sound.

'I heard one of the servants say something,' I lie.

'Rubbish. I only had you two girls. Did your father say this to you?' she asks.

'No! No!' I reply quickly. I don't want my father to get reprimanded for something he never said to me. I don't want to tell her that N Dead and Saralama have both told me this.

'Do you know I got kidnapped once?' she says suddenly.

A story from Anima, herself. That is a rare thing.

I can feel N Dead hovering over us, waiting for my mother to begin her story. Later, I am sure, she will tell me her version and fill in the gaps. Her memory is sharper because she often goes back into those very places. My mother has to tell her story by only relying on what is stored in her mind. All ordinary people can only do that, while I have N Dead to take me to the exact place in her memories.

I have realized that there are so many layers to the same story my mother and N Dead tell me. Each one wants to add something of herself and then the kernel of truth begins to dissolve. N Dead brings her own scent, nuggets of her own perspective to the tale while my mother, a gifted storyteller, goes higher and deeper into her imagination; embellishing her story with lies. Each woman loves to embroider with words and swiftly their fingers fly over the story—a flower here, a haunted house there. It will soon be my story and I can then walk over their words and quietly weave myself into the story. Once you hear a story it is forever yours. You can add to it, you can forget it, or remember it all your life.

[Excerpted from the author's forthcoming novel, *Travels With My Beloved Ghost.*]

Publisher's Acknowledgements

The Publishers acknowledge with thanks permission to reproduce the following stories:

1. 'Rites of Passage', excerpted from *In Other Words, New Writings* by Indian Women, Ed. Urvashi Butalia and Ritu Menon, published by Kali for Women, 1992.
2. 'Toofan', excerpted from *The Perfect Woman: Short Stories*, pub. UBSPD, 1994.
3. 'Food to Die For', excerpted from *Anger of the Aubergines*, published by Women Unlimited, 1997/2005.
4. 'The Pink Velvet Dressing Gown', excerpted from *A Second Skin: Women Write About Clothes*, Ed. Kirsty Dunseath, published by Women's Press, UK, 1998.
5. 'Anadi's Journey', excerpted from *A Storehouse of Tales: Contemporary Indian Women Writers,* Ed. Jehanara Wasi, published by Srishti Publishers, 2001.

6. 'Hiding Away', excerpted from *Days of Innocence: Stories for Ruskin Bond*, Namita Gokhale Editions, published by Roli Books, 2002.
7. 'Lost Garden', excerpted from Namaste Magazine, Vol. XXIX/1 and 2, 2009; 'In Possession', Namaste Magazine, Vol. XXX/2-3, 2011-12.
8. 'Friends Forever', excerpted from *A Clear Blue Sky: Stories and Poems on Conflict and Hope*, published by Puffin Books, Penguin India, 2010.
9. 'Revenge in Thread', excerpted from *Eating Women, Telling Tales,* published by Zubaan, 2013.
10. 'Mayadevi's London Yatra', 'To Shimla in a Tonga' and 'Trials of a Tall Aunt', excerpted from *Travels with My Aunts*, published by Women Unlimited, 2015.
11. 'The Child-thief', excerpted from *It's All Connected: Feminist Fiction and Poetry*, Ed. Pauline Hopkins, published by Spinifex Press, UK, 2022.